Creative Survival

Library of Congress cataloging data
Azel Adams, author
Sally K. Butcher, editor
Creative Survival: A Narrative History of Azel Adams,
The Forks, Maine.
Library of Congress Number 91-68485
ISBN 0-9631912-1-7

Old Bess Publishing Co.
P. O. Box 297
Brunswick, ME 04011

Creative Survival

*A Narrative History of
Azel Adams, The Forks, Maine.*

Compiled by Sally K. Butcher

Old Bess Publishing Co.
Brunswick, Maine

Foreward

He was a blacksmith's apprentice, a bootlegger, lumber camp cook, river driver and Maine guide. He could handle a horse and wagon while still a child. He visited the summer hunting camps of Maine Indians before their migrations became history, and he suffered the hardships of people who live life at the edge.

Azel Adams, a long time resident of Richmond, Maine, never set out to collect a lifetime of maverick experiences. Born on a twenty-acre farm in a town called The Forks in northwestern Maine, the son of a guide and trapper and farm wife with a genius for survival, Adams' early life was a kind of anachronism. While a growing urban America hurled toward the hustle and bustle of contemporary life, Adams came of age in a kind of American backwater, learning pioneer skills used during the previous 300 years of America's settlement. Skills like preserving meat at the bottom of a well, shoeing horses, cooking for lumbermen in isolated camps.

To be sure, Adams' life as a latter day pioneer was not unique in northern New England. Before paved roads and the whole Interstate system opened the most isolated parts of the country to sportsmen and tourists, people like Adams used their wits and skill to design their own creative survival. What is unique about Adams is his marvelous recall; his wonderful ability to paint the picture of a life now vanished from Maine and all of New England.

With respect for her subject and the fascinating story he relates, Sally Butcher has made a valuable contribution to the history of Maine.

But CREATIVE SURVIVAL does more than document early 20th Century life in a particular rural place. It shows how humor thrives with adversity, how personal loyalty and family togetherness overcome obstacles and — most of all—how wide and various life in America once was.

Lloyd Ferriss
President, Richmond Historical Society

PREFACE

Azel Adams was born in The Forks, Maine, in 1912. The Forks is located at the confluence of the Kennebec River and Dead River and on the old Canada Road, now U.S. 201. It is roughly half way between Portland and Quebec City.

When Mr. Adams was a boy, thirty or forty families lived in the town. In the summer and fall, fishermen and hunters patronized the local hotels and sporting camps. Many were "moneyed people" who stayed several weeks or months, and guiding these people provided employment for the men in the town. During the winter and spring, lumbering and trapping were the main employment.

Now the town is smaller. Thirty or forty people are year-round residents. Fishermen and hunters still come, but most have their own camps. The town has a few small inns and bed and breakfasts, but no large hotel. The greatest number of tourists come for white water rafting and stay for only a few days. There are twelve rafting companies located in The Forks, and during the summer of 1991, twenty-nine thousand people rafted the Kennebec.

I first met Mr. Adams in the early 1970's when I needed parts for a wood burning cookstove. Since then I have bought and traded several stoves, partly because dealing with Azel is a great pleasure. One day he remarked that not only had many of the arts that he had learned as a "child growing up to live off the Maine woods" disappeared, but the obligation that the elders felt to teach the young their crafts had vanished. That whole way of life had gone forever. He noted that having begun in The Forks, and equipped with only a high school education, he had gone on to supervise huge construction projects. Maybe someone should write a book.

So during the winter of 1984, and since, Azel and I have sat in his kitchen or living room in Richmond, Maine, and he has told me about his life. We have about twenty ninety-minute tapes which I have transcribed and condensed to the following narrative. I have left out a great deal. With the exception of two or three short comments by Mrs. Adams, all the words are those of Azel Adams. This is a transcription of his oral history.

Imagine yourself in the warm kitchen having a "lunch" of coffee, donuts and cheddar cheese, or comfortably ensconced in the living room, learning about the ways of the past and the remarkable way that this family has dealt with the changing times.

Read and enjoy.

Sally K. Butcher, 1991.

Acknowledgements

The photo of Azel Adams on the back cover is by Lloyd Ferriss. The drawings of calk boots, the smoking barrel and hewing a log are by Thomas Spande. All other photos, unless otherwise noted, are from Azel Adams's collection.

I have had help from many people , including Polly Greason, John Ladley, Richard Morgan, Frank Burroughs, Judy Foster and Liz Pierson. But my greatest help has been from my husband, Sam.

CHAPTER ONE

Early Days

I was the fourth child in the family. There was three girls prior so that when I come along they thought that was a big thing. There was a girl and four boys after me, and there was another boy, but he died at birth. Ten children in all. I was born August 8, 1912.

We were brought up on a farm, about twenty acres, in The Forks, Maine. You are acquainted with the Marshall House. That house on the hill, south of the hotel, I was brought up there. My father was a game warden when I was born but then he gave that up. A warden was paid two dollars a day in those days, and a guide was getting four dollars a day, so he took up guiding, working in the woods in the winter, trapping. The family kept growing and there was always work for my father.

There isn't three acres clear land where the old house sits on the hill there now. My brother Clyde he owns it now. We tried to fix the old home back as Mother used to have it... The stove that she had, that's going back. My brother Oliver had it first, and he sold it to my brother Clyde.

So, being of a large family, we always had to work. We used to mow the hay and then rake it. The whole family'd turn out. The farm was so rocky and rough you had to mow it by hand. You had to be an artist with a scythe in order to keep from hitting the rocks. We put the hay in the haycocks. If it dried enough on the first day we'd load it in the hayracks that we'd haul behind the horses and take it into the barn and pitch it into the mows.

We raised sheep too on that farm and I always said when I was a kid when the other kids would be playing baseball or playing marbles in front of the local store in the spring of the year, I'd have to stay home and hold the lambs up by their hind feet so they could feed down between the rocks. 'Course a lot of people don't think that is quite so, and it is probably elaborating a little bit, but that's the way I felt.

The sheep we used to have in what we called the back pastures. Years ago back at the turn of the century, there was a road along the Kennebec River like there is now around Wyman Lake that was known as the Frost Road, but the main road, the road we used most, that road used to be on the height of land and it was known as the Military Road. As you're going up from Bingham going north to Caratunk you can look up on the hill on the right hand side and you can see old farms up there. Well those farms used to be on the road that went from Bingham to right back of the Marshall Hotel, at The Forks, and they called it twenty-five miles then. Back of our place was what we called the Burnham lot, that was a beautiful big farm and field, then there was the Durgin Farm, McNealy Farm, the Jim Stewart Farm. These was all within the town of The Forks. And as you go further south you come over into other farms. That was the only way to Bingham.

These farms was very rich with strawberries, blueberries, gooseberries, currants, apple trees. The old timers had to have all these for a living. In the spring of the year when the first fruits were ready Mother would take us children, pack a lunch, and we'd head for the McNealy field or the Jim Stewart field and we'd stay all day and pick our berries. The Durgin field, right back of our place, we'd keep that fenced for the sheep.

Mother'd say, "You fill this pail. And there is no fooling and there's no playing until you get your pails full."

Whatever there was, everybody helped. Putting in the garden, weeding the garden. You didn't say, "I don't want to." You never gained anything.

In being raised by a woman like my mother, you didn't leave that house until you had the basic education of living. Some people call it hard, but we knew how to cook, we knew how to do everything. We was taught the value of the earth. Every herb that come through the ground could be used. It was there for us. If we didn't know it we might be sorry. Everybody had his own thing to do. We'd all go strawberrying, or raspberrying, and we'd go as a group, a family.

Along there by the Marshall Hotel we had a swimming hole. We even rocked places around so that we'd have dead water in there. There was a little bit of sand, gravel. There was a rock there that we'd dive off of. Get up on that rock and look down and you'd see five or six big suckers swimming along and they were heading up the river then. Suckers run up in the Spring. We could hardly wait for a feed of fiddlehead greens, a feed of suckers. We used to go down to the river and catch them. Go barefoot. I think we were about the only family around that ate suckers. We had a spear, and we'd go right down to that same rock that we used to dive off and we'd spear these suckers. They weren't wormy. They was right up there in that mountain spring water. We'd take them home, scale them, leave their head on, clean them out, put them in a barrel of salt brine, leave them about two days and then put them in the smoke house. We would smoke them eight, ten hours and take the heads and tails off, and pack them away in boxes with wax paper, put them where it was cool. Then in the summer months we'd have new potatoes out of the garden, and go down and get one or two of them suckers. Mother would skin them, bone them, put them in the oven, make a nice egg sauce with them. Good eating, good living.

About half way between The Forks and Jackman is Lake Parlin, and the Lake Parlin Farm was owned by the Piels Brewery. My dad built some camps down on the lake for Mrs. Lang. She was a Piel. Later he built a couple of

Lake Parlin House. Lake Parlin, Maine
Bangor and Aroostook Railroad. *In the Pine Tree Jungles.*
Bangor, Maine 1929.

camps in at Lang Pond over the mountain across Parlin
so she and her family could go in and stay summers.
North of the farm on the right, there used to be a big
hotel, the Parlin Hotel. It was owned by H. P. MacKinney,
and he was quite an industrious man in those days and
well thought of. They used to say that the hotel was
halfway between Portland and Quebec City. That was
the halfway point and they would advertise it that way.

I was nine years old when I started to work. Mother
drove me up there to the hotel, dropped me off the day
after school let out. She gave me a dollar and a half.
She'd filled out two or three postcards she wanted me to
mail and I'd just mail them in, sometimes with nothing

written on them.

I had the job of working in the laundry, turning the mangle, turning the wringer, nothing was electric then. I had a cart to haul the clothes out. They was all dried on lines then. I worked there seventy-two days and I come home. I hired out for a dollar a day. When they paid me off I had seventy-two dollars to bring home, and my mother had given me a dollar and a half and I had about a dollar of that and I had about four or five dollars where that I had got tips. Those days we worked from six in the morning till six at night. That was 1921.

When I come home I gave my mother twenty-five dollars of that money to buy groceries and things for the home. We had a 1922 Chevrolet. It had just come out. Baby Grand, made in Canada; it was bigger than the regular Chevrolets. We went down to Bingham, twenty-three miles, and we went into the grocery store there, bought a barrel of flour, two dollars and a half. Hundred pounds of beans, four cents a pound, four dollars. Twenty gallons of molasses, fifteen cents a gallon. Twenty-five dollars overloaded that automobile.

We put the top down and that back seat was full. That twenty-five dollars was all the staple food that we had to have for that winter. Beans, molasses, flour and sugar - staples that you couldn't raise on the farm. That left me a little money.

Mother bought me a Nash suit. We ordered it by mail, twenty dollars, because I was under fifteen. Over fifteen you had to pay twenty-five.

Of course, during the winter I went to school. We

always had the chores of cutting the wood, the ice, and cutting the hay, as well as taking care of the cows, horses and hogs. Today people put a value to that but we didn't. This was a necessity. You talk with people today they say, "Well, you can't afford it. You can't do it today." It's no different today than it was then. It was the attitude you had toward working. Everybody thinks now that they're sitting down drinking coffee they should be getting paid, that that's a necessity more than living.

This fellow that owned the Lake Parlin Hotel, H. P. MacKinney, was made road commissioner that next spring. He was to build a good automobile road through the town of The Forks and up through Jackman. I had worked for him the summer before at the hotel and I asked him for a job on the road. He put me to work raking rocks on the road on the finished part. Dollar and a half a day and I stayed home. You were never paid by the hour, you were paid by the day and the days then run ten hours a day. You had no coffee breaks; you had a half hour to eat your dinner and that was it.

Well I worked on the road through summer vacation. I used to work nights for an hour or so over at the Marshall House. Fred Marshall was the fellow who owned the hotel. He'd let me over there, and whatever he'd be doing, I'd ask questions and want to get into it and help him. He took me in hand this way. He was soldering once, and I said, "Will you show me how to do that?"

"Yes," he says, "I'll show you, but you're going to

have to pay attention. I'm not going to do it a half dozen times."

And he showed me how. I've been dedicated to him all my life for the things he taught me and what he done for me.

I didn't realize it at the time but my knowledge of soldering and metal and everything is largely owed to men like him. My grandfather on my mother's side was a blacksmith and two uncles on my father's side was blacksmiths. So I was in their shops. I learned how to cock up shoes for horses or oxen, or iron a sled, and I was doing this when I was twelve, thirteen years old. We learned because we had to do everything ourselves. Today, people never have that chance to learn. I had it and I profited by it. It was the biggest help in later years when I worked in construction. I found in the large jobs that most of my good men had been farm boys or come out of the woods where a man had to make changes fast and know what he was doing. It was good for us to learn that way.

I said in the winter of course we went to school. Well, there used to be a grammar school downstairs and a high school up, and that used to accommodate the children from West Forks, The Forks, and Lake Moxie.

I was thinking the other day of a family that lived in Moxie. The father was a railroad section foreman. There was three boys and one girl. It's six miles from Moxie out to that school. Those children going to high school would have to walk. For a while there was one family that had a driving horse and the kids used to come out by sleigh in the winter. Later on one of the boys in his last year of high school bought an old 1924 Essex sedan and he used to haul the kids. But mostly in the winter months they'd ski out. It's more down hill from Moxie to The Forks and they used to come out there six miles in an hour. Those kids never missed any school. Rain, cold, snow storms, anything, they still would go. Now we have to furnish the kids a bus and after they get to school we have to furnish them somebody to make them exercise... a big gymnasium.

There was an old outside privy at this school that set out by a ledge. The ledge went up and the doors faced the ledge. You had just about room to go between the ledge and the house to get in there. Well, they'd laid new hardwood flooring in the school and they had what was left over by the privy in a pile. The principal, the only teacher they had for about thirty-five, forty kids, he'd gone into the privy. The toilet door used to open in with a big large handle. One of the older boys run a board through the handle and across the door and the principal couldn't come out. The principal stuck his head out a little old square window, no glass in it, at the end of the toilet, and he was hollering and threatening the kids if they didn't unlock that door. Well there was boys there that was men grown that was in the eighth grade. Quite a few.

"Let's tip the toilet over with him in it!"

So we went along. It was a two holer for boys, and there was two holes for the girls too, all in the same privy. But all of the kids got together and we tipped it up against the ledge. Then we run.

The principal threatened us that we'd lose all our recesses for the rest of the year, which we did.

I was only six or seven years old when that happened. I wouldn't have done anything like that anyway.

This same teacher used to go down and eat at a farmhouse down below, right in sight of the school. And he'd leave one older kid in charge. Usually it was a girl. One year they'd cut the hay during the summer around there and there was haycocks near the school. There was a tree that grew right up beside the schoolhouse, and this kid, Norman Gilpatrick, went up there and got on to the roof.

He said, "Bring up some of that hay."

So we started getting that hay up to him on the roof and he'd carry it over and push it down the chimney. He plugged that chimney right plumb full of hay. It was two or three weeks before we built a fire in that stove and when we did all the smoke come out into the room. The teacher had to send us home. So we was catching on and we was thinking of everything that we could do to get sent home from school. Wonder we didn't burn the schoolhouse down. I wasn't always the instigator , but I was usually among the group.

The West Forks Hotel was eight miles north of the Kennebec River on the road to Jackman, and it was run by Tom Berry, my grandfather on my mother's side. It was eight, ten rooms. Across the road he had a livery stable, blacksmith shop, jewelery shop, barber shop, and he used to doctor the horses.

I used to beg to go up there in the winter. I was only about five years old, I guess. One of my uncles or my aunts would take me up. My grandfather used to work eighteen hours a day. He'd be making horseshoes ahead. He made them out of straight bars of iron. He used to wrap me up in a horse blanket, take me out to the shop. He had the big bellows to run the forge and the rope hung down from the handle right beside where he stood. He'd put me up there by the fire wrapped up in a horse blanket and let me pull the bellows. I was so proud! I'll never forget it.

He was welding cocks on the shoes and when he hit it the sparks flew everywhere. One of them hit and went up my nose. Of course it burnt. Oh, I howled some wicked. He takes me into the house.

"Well, it's time to quit anyway. We'll have some tea."

I was five years old and he poured me a little cup of tea.

He said, "We'll eat some squeaky bisquits and butter."

Dry old bisquits. He liked them. He'd slice them off and put a little butter on them and we'd set there. I forgot about being burnt and all that.

To cock up a shoe for horse or ox, he'd have these bars of iron that he'd pound out. The shoe had a toe cock and two heel cocks. He'd weld the pieces on and when he did he'd have to have that iron right to a melting heat. If ever you hear of a man going with a horse and he'd say he broke a toe cock off, anyone listening'd say, "Who was the blacksmith?"

You'd never hear of one of Tom Berry's coming off. He was a metallurgist. He knew his irons. He didn't read it in books, he didn't study it, he learned it on his own.

I recall as a kid, seven or eight years old, being in the local grocery store. Used to be some tourists come up to there, have a camp and stay a while. They come in by train to Moxie and the stage would bring them to The Forks. It used to be an old Stanley Steamer that would meet the trains and haul people around to the different places. Well, these people had been there all summer and somebody was sick in the family and the nearest doctor was twenty-three miles away. They was in the grocery store and there was a fellow by the name of Mont Bean had a car that he used to haul people, and my grandfather had one. It was a Reo and it had curtains. It was getting to the fall of the year and I heard this Mr. Holway say, "If you're going to get one, they're both good, reliable people, but I think you'd be warmer, it's getting cool now, Tom Berry's car has got curtains on it."

So this was the big selling point, and I was just as proud as a kid to think that my grandfather had the best automobile in town. There was only about three or four automobiles in the town.

The way the gasoline came then was in forty-five gallon steel drums from the railhead, and they used to pour it out into five gallon cans and then take a funnel and fill your car up. Kerosene for your lights.

Those days in the local grocery store I seen the first loaf of bread that ever come into that town. The bread would come in great big boxes with paper lined inside but the loaves were not wrapped. They stood on end in there with a cover over them. And then they'd put them in a show case in the store. A woman was a lazy person if she couldn't make her own bread. Anybody buying a loaf of bread never was a woman, it was a man living alone or something. Those days are gone.

Back in the days when I was seven to ten to twelve years old there was a fellow by the name of Leo Fournier that was in charge of the Hollingsworth and Whitney lumbering operation and the Cold Stream Depot Camp. Out from the depot camp they'd probably have six or seven camps with anywhere from hundred to a hundred and fifty men in each camp cutting pulpwood. In those days if you didn't put ice up you didn't keep much in the way of food. Stuff being shipped wasn't shipped with ice. And so it became either all canned stuff or you had to stock fresh meat right there.

I recall a fellow name Sherm Gonier had a contract for furnishing the beef for the lumber camps. He used to get us young fellows to help him drive the cows. Probably start down at Skowhegan, then forty-five miles to The Forks and then it was further than that up to Cold Stream. You might have twenty head of cattle or you might have only ten or might be only five. You couldn't hurry them, you had to let them feed along the road. I might be on this trip, or my sister and I or another young fellow and myself. We'd drive them during the day, and when the cows'd bed down at night, Mr. Gonier would pick us up and take us home. In the morning we'd go back.

Well, when it got time to kill the cattle in the camps, somebody would have to go up and butcher them. So Father would go up and help. I think he used to get fifty cents a head, and get the livers and the heart. And all he'd do was shoot them and take the innards out and skin them out. And they had men to help do that. So Father would bring down the livers and the hearts and he'd sell them to the local grocery store or might take them home.

They always raised the pigs right behind the cook camps. Fed them from the waste from the camps, and a lot of the pigs ran wild in the woods. They got loose. The leaf of the fat on the pig and the heads they didn't want in the camps. So Father would bring them home and Mother'd make hog's head cheese or she'd make scrapple. From that leaf fat they used to make the soap. Lye soap.

Mother would have a fire and a kettle outdoors. If she wanted to make soap she'd boil that lard with lye and everything and put it in these big pans. We used to call them sap pans. After it cooled and hardened they'd cut it and the different women around the town, they'd say, "Boy, that's awful good soap you made, Leena."

Then they started getting some scents to put into it to make it smell good, like the boughten soap, but people couldn't afford the boughten soap. This was about the time the first loaf of bread come into the store.

I was recalling my home life as a kid growing up. We ate more venison and lamb or veal than we did beef. In fact I didn't acquire a taste for beef until I was away from home when you couldn't get venison all the time. My father always said and I maintain too that venison is at its best when it was killed in the month of August.

We were talking the other day about dry beef, chipped beef, jerky, what not. My father used to have a method of making his own jerky, making it out of venison. I was too young to know what he had in the brine that he'd soak it in but he'd take a whole hind quarter of venison and he'd bone it out. Then he'd take a wood skewer, poke holes into the meat, and put it in that brine for about a week. Then we had an old hand cider press. He'd put the venison in that and wind her down to get it dry. And he'd tell us, "Anybody going by, see if you can take a little turn on that handle."

Well, after he'd pressed all the liquid out of the meat, he'd poke a hole through it and put a string in it, take it and hang it up in the culvert that went underneath the road. It was a big wood culvert and you could walk through it. It had the sleeper logs there that carried the weight, and there was a bunch of nails in the sleeper logs.

I recall this one time, I was just a young fellow, him taking that meat down and hanging it up in the culvert right in the summer. Wind blowing through, right over the spring water, cool, no flies. He'd leave that there for a month, just drying. When we'd go in the woods when we were trapping or anything, we'd chop some of that off and take it with us.

One time, it was in the latter part of August, a big buck that had strayed too close to the house become part of our larder. So Mother, after it was all skun out, she took this deer meat and sliced it up. We had those wooden lard tubs, we called them twenty-pound lard tubs, and they used to have a cover on them. She took one of them, she set it down on the hearth in front of the old wood stove and she had a fry pan with lard in it, melted. Then she had another one with lard in it but it was real hot. I can see those platters of steak. She'd take a fork of that steak and dip it into that boiling lard and just sear it all over. Then she'd put it in the other tub, putting on lard that was just barely melted. She filled that tub right up with venison covered with lard, let it cool off. When it was ready we took it about a hundred yards back of the house to a spring. There was about a three-foot tile in the ground in that spring. We tied rope around the tub and lowered it into the water.

I recall my uncle from Vermont come over in October and wanted to know if we had any venison. Mother sent my sister and me up with a dish and fork and a knife and she told us to get seven or eight big slices of that venison. We pulled it up from the spring, cut the lard, got the steak and brought it down. She took that venison and dipped it in boiling water, held it up and put it in the fry pan to cook. You know I don't think you could even taste that lard. The steak had just been seared on the outside and that grease, that cooler lard had kept the bacteria away. I know we kept venison steak like that a month and a half, two months.

Then my mother used to can venison. We used to buy Libby's cans of roast beef, but she could can venison so much better than Libby's or those people. I don't know if it was better, probably it was my appetite or my taste was accustomed to what we had at home. I can recall my having beef steak and not liking it because it was too greasy.

My mother always made mincemeat from venison. This is the recipe we use now.

The juice of three oranges, three lemons. The grated rind of one orange and one lemon. Quart of molasses, quart of vinegar and two bags of apples. A yellow bowl of ground venison (about half the volume of apples), and the liquid that the meat cooked in. Four or five pounds of raisins, a can of peaches and all the spices. Two pounds suet, ground up fine. Simmer very carefully.

This makes fourteen quarts of venison mincemeat. She (my wife) says to put in a pint of brandy after it's all made. I generally put in a fifth.

Before and during World War One, alders was used to make gun powder, and this was one of the industries that we had at that time. Any family had many alders could get some money. We would go into the alder swamps and cut the trees and pile them up. When the first snow would come we would haul them with the teams out to the railhead and load them in a coal car. The trees were shipped then to DuPont down in Delaware. They were used in making gun powder.

In those days there was values in a lot of stuff. But there was work with all of it.

My father was taken sick with the flu that went around, 1922, 23. Everybody in the family had the flu, but he was the first to come down with it. Well, as the rest come down, and mother had to go to bed - this was the year my kid sister was born, she was born in October - he got up out of bed and took care of us when he should have been in bed recovering. It left him with problems with his lungs. They wanted to send him to a sanitorium but he didn't want to go so they built him a little house that he lived in. They didn't want him near us children because at that time they didn't have the methods to find out if he had TB or what. We all got better but my father never really recovered.

My father when he was sick everytime he'd cough he was spitting blood and in bad shape, and there wasn't too much to eat on the farm.

Mother says, "I'm goin' hunting tomorrow morning, up on the old Will Holway field."

It had apple trees and it wasn't too far back there.

We had an old rifle, an old twenty-five thirty-five carbine. She takes that and puts on a pair of Father's rubbers, heavy pants, and she takes off to go hunting. Gone about two hours. There was a little bit of snow on the ground and me and my sister Claudia we were thinking about going up and finding her. We knew that Father was a little nervous, he was walking around and kept looking out the window, and he could hardly get around, he was so weak.

Looked up over the hill and here come Mother out into the bushes, out of the field, dragging something behind her. Well, we knew she had a deer. When she came in down back of the barn she stopped there. Then she come into the house, big grin on her face.

Father says, "What'd you get?"

She says, "I got three of them. I got an old doe and two lambs." She says, "They haven't been dressed off yet, Will."

She had taken the belt offen her pants, put it around the old doe's neck, tied it so she'd have something to drag the deer with. It was all down hill and there was snow on the ground. She'd taken the shoe laces out of each shoe, tied it around the little lambs' necks and tied them to the hind legs of the old doe and dragged them all home.

Father says to me, "You go over to the hotel, and you see Billy King, and tell him I'd like to have him come over right away."

Billy come over and Father told him he'd like to have him dress them deer out. Billy dressed them off and he hung them in the barn. Next day he come over and he skun them out. Now I'm telling you that was a big help for meat for the family. What ever we killed we had a use for. We lived offen the woods.

My father was a warden when he and my mother got married in 1906, and he was a warden for about five or six years. Then he quit and got into guiding to get more money to support the family. He guided, trapped and worked in the woods. He was away from home most of the time, working in the lumber camps or in the sporting camps guiding or trapping. I worked trapping with him when I was about fifteen, sixteen.

We had two dogs and a sled, and they'd haul fifty, sixty pounds. We'd take our traps and head out. We'd be gone all week.

I recall we had a camp in on Ten Thousand Acres at Ellis Pond, and we'd stay in that two nights. The rest of the time we were sleeping in lean-tos in the woods, twenty, forty below zero sometimes. We banked the bough lean-to up. Father knew how to fix a fire against a ledge and it would reflect in and Father and I and two dogs would crawl in there and sleep. We done that for about four or five weeks, trapping, every winter.

One particular winter we got over a hundred beaver. At that time blanket beaver was going for a dollar an inch. It had to be 72 inches. The other beaver would average twenty to thirty dollars apiece. And we used to pick up a few mink. I always had the muskrat that we'd catch for my spending money. I got an otter once in a mink trap. He drowned is what happened. At that time you'd get ninety dollars for an otter.

All in all this way of living didn't help my dad. I didn't realize at the time that he'd never really got over the flu. A lot of things you don't know until you get out and away from home. It's a way of living. In fact I didn't realize we were poor people. We was just as happy with what we had and we always found a way to get by and make do. Thanks to my mother. I don't think there are many women that could do what she could.

My father used to make scents for trappers. All he had was an eight by eight shack up on the hill that he'd go into when he was actually bottling the scent. He'd take a skunk and not draw any scent at all.

If there was any horse meat available or a beef critter or something he'd get the meat and cut it all up in little fine pieces and he'd put it in a jug. The two ends of the scent bag from the skunk would be tied up. He'd throw that into the jug. He was very careful not to be touching it with his hands. Then he let that set and rot right out in the sun. That cap tight. He'd punch a hole with a nail in the top. He'd take something like a sharp wire, go down there and punch that scent bag, stir it all up, pull the wire out and put a piece of sealing wax over the hole and seal it up. Shake the jug up, leave it there.

He'd buy them little bottles, they was square and a tight stopper in them and he would fill them. That's when it would stink and he'd go up there in that shack, put on some old clothes and fill the bottles. He used to sell them for a dollar seventy-five, two dollars a bottle. I imagine L.L.Bean might have bought some back in those days. He used to make a lot of it. For mink, he'd put fish, catch some chubs, cut them all up and put them in. Different baits he had. Now wildcat he always said was the hardest thing there was. He used to use deer meat on that. He always used the skunk scent as the carrier.

Back in those days there was two Indians would come to town during the summer months. One, Mr. Francis, and the other we called Paul. They came every year for five or six years. They would set up near a brook and pitch a tent or makeshift camp. They had very little food around. They lived on a lot of greens and herbs from the woods - they'd pick what we called cow slips, lily of the valley, fiddleheads - and rabbits.

My mother would give me a two-quart pail of milk to take to Mr. Francis and he'd put it in the brook to keep cool. He used to make us bows and arrows. He taught us how to make slingshots and set snares for rabbits. There were some of us young folks they would let visit and help them make baskets, and they made paddles and axe handles, all out of ash.

The flies never seemed to bother them. They would pick sweet grass and sarsaparilla along the brook. They would wear it around their heads and have a small smudge pot going and they would put a small sprig of sarsaparilla in the pot. When we had a lot of flies around home we used to ask to go visit the Indians as they never had flies.

There used to be a huge Indian burial mound in The Forks, and before anyone knew what it was we would use the rocks to fill holes on the road. We dug and hauled rocks out of there for a long time, and it was after I was married for a couple of years and I was living in Jackman that I heard on the radio that a burial ground had been found at The Forks.

So I went home one day and I went and looked at it. The road crew had opened up the pile and had found three or four burial holes or pockets and there was arrow heads and spears in there. I don't know if they ever found any bones. I do know that Mr. Merrill, it was in his pasture, put signs "Keep Off" and charged twenty-five cents for people to go in and look at the pile. But he didn't take care of it, have somebody there watching it, and people was taking artifacts out of there and stealing stuff.

Mr. Francis and Paul camped not over four hundred yards from that burial ground. They said then, "This is our home."

They used to tell us kids that they was there long before we were. I've often wondered if they actually knew that that was a burial ground. As a kid I played on that rock pile and I thought that the farmers had just gathered the rocks and put them there from their fields.

On a point near where the Dead River and the Kennebec come together there had been a big Indian camp ground. I recall when I was seven, eight years old, I used to go over there with Carl Sandburg who married my cousin Hazel Durgin. He was a professor and he'd come up on his vacations from Connecticut. He used to go over there and dig. He'd take us kids and get us hoes and he'd get a pile of arrowheads. Not only arrow heads, but spear heads and axes, and he'd explain this to us kids. It didn't mean anything to us. We thought he was crazy getting all that stuff. But at one time it must have been a big campground.

About the same time the Indians were coming to town the Gypsies would come. They would come in caravans of four to ten autos, most of them old and large. The Gypsies would have all their possessions, hens, goats and dogs. Everyone was on the lookout because they would go into the pastures and milk the cows and steal the hens. One of the natives went into his barn to milk and caught two of these women milking a cow. He was going to have them arrested but they told the sheriff the farmer had told them they could have the milk. So the case was dropped as the farmer had no witness.

We always cut our own wood to home. When you got ready to saw your wood into stove-size pieces, saw it and split it, you used to have "bees." The fellow that owned the sawing machine was the only fellow that got paid. He got a dollar a cord. You'd have a bee, you might have five or six men there lifting the logs, lifting the logs.

When we got ready to cut our wood to home we had about fifteen cords. So this one time they brought the sawing machine in at night and the fellow that owned the sawing machine had lost a bolt out of the arbor on the saw. Well, the set screw that should have been in the arbor of that saw would have set flush, but it had come out and he didn't have one to put back in. So the fellow screwed in a bolt about three inches long and it was sticking out right up next to the saw. He'd cut a groove in the table so the bolt wouldn't hit it as it went around.

I was big for my age and rugged - I was thirteen years old - so I was throwing the wood away from the saw after each cut. Well about ten o'clock in the morning we was sawing a large maple log and I had hold of it, ready to take it, and it didn't quite saw off. The fellow give it another push and when he did, my hand got caught. That's what I got. Both fingers.

Well, when I come into the house, into the kitchen, Mother was just putting potatoes on for dinner and I reached down, grabbed a potato and put it under my arm. I had just studied pressure points a week or so before in school. Mother wrapped my hand up.

Well, it was winter and in those days we was twenty-three miles from a doctor. There was a fellow named Eddie Comber had a snowmobile and they called him. It was not the type of snowmobile they use now, it was a real automobile with lags on it and runners.

So Mother, Father, Eddie and myself, we headed out. We left The Forks about eleven o'clock, we got down to Bingham about four thirty, five o'clock. Had a flat tire on the thing inside of the lag on the way.

So anyway, when we got into Bingham we looked up the old doctor.

He said, "I've got to give him ether."

The fellow that owned the snowmobile, Ed, said he could help. They laid me down and put the mask over my face. The doctor unwrapped my hand. Well this fellow see the blood, and it bothered him. I could hear him say, "I'm going to leave you," and he hit the floor. So mother had to assist the doctor to give me ether, cut my fingers off and fix up my hand.

Another fellow that had problems with a saw was Mr. Marshall, that had the Marshall House. He had what they call an Ottawa drag saw to saw his wood. He had called my grandfather who was a blacksmith to build a guard over the top of this set of gears. Mr. Marshall started the saw and he was showing my grandfather the break in the casting. He had just put water in the engine and the weather was cold. He had got water on his leather mittens, and when he went down to thrust the saw to stop, his hand froze to the gear and it took his hand off right at the wrist.

This happened just a year prior to when I lost my fingers, and they didn't have the snowmobile in the area then. I don't remember myself, but I've heard that Grandfather put a tourniquet on Mr. Marshall's arm and bandaged it up and he bundled Mr. Marshall up in the big robes and took him to Bingham. My mother went with them. Twenty-three miles to Bingham and that pair of horses of my grandfather's had already come about eight miles to get to The Forks.

The doctor, who was the same doctor that took care of my fingers, told me, he said, "If it hadn't been for Tom Berry," that was my grandfather, "Fred Marshall would have bled to death before he got here."

My grandfather come back and took the hand up to the gravel pit, dug a hole and buried it. Mr. Marshall was in the hospital and he was complaining about his hand aching. So the doctor called the people next door to Marshall's, Sandy Harris, and asked if he knew where the hand was.

"No," he says, "but I think I can find it." He says, "Snow on the ground, I'll follow Tom Berry's tracks."

So Sandy went up to the gravel pit and he see where my grandfather had buried it. He put the hand in a box, shoe box, brought it down and he called back down to the hospital, told the doctor that he had the hand, what did the doctor want him to do with it.

"Well," says the doctor, "you build a good fire in the furnace or something and you put that hand in and burn it."

So that's what Sandy did. Mr. Marshall said he never had any more trouble with that hand.

Well, when I had my accident, these fingers and my hand was wrapped up in a pillowcase. We didn't have a lot of bandages or anything. So when we got to the doctor's he unwrapped my hand and when he cut these fingers off he laid them on the pillowcase.

My mother and I went down and stayed with my sister. Father and the fellow with the snowmobile went back to The Forks.

That night it started raining. We had one heck of a thaw. This doctor's office was upstairs. There was a roof of an addition, and you lift the window up and there was the roof, right there. Well it was probably six, seven at night before he got done with me and he just wrapped the fingers in the pillowcase, put it in a basket and slid it out the window, under the eaves.

Now I don't know why it was, but I woke up in the night and that hand was freezing! So cold, felt like sharp piercing cold going through it. Well, I woke my mother and she come in and I told her. I went downstairs and it was raining hard. From where my sister lived to where the doctor was was less than a quarter of a mile.

So at six o'clock in the morning my mother says, "Well, the doctor better be up now. So I will call."

She called.

She said, "Something's wrong." She says, "He can't stand the pain."

The doctor said, "Well, bring him up."

I went up to him about six thirty or seven o'clock. He come into his office, he unbandaged my hand, looked it all over and said, "I don't see a thing wrong."

He talked to my mother. He said, "Oh, do you want to take your pillow slips and your stuff back?"

Mother said, "Yes."

He put up the window and he brought them in. He said, "I'm going to take care of something."

He took them fingers and he went downstairs and he put them into the furnace or something and my hand stopped aching. Now, I don't tell many people that because they think I'm crazy.

Creative Survival

CHAPTER TWO

High School Years

My mother thought that when we went to school, we had to go with little white shirts on and a necktie and we had to have our hair combed and even though our pants would have patches over patches, we had to look neat and clean.

Well, I was in my junior year in high school and the teacher had mentioned two or three times about people copying other people's work. The teacher put an exam on the board and we was writing our answers. This fellow that set with me in the double seat was in my class, and he leaned right over and he was looking at my work. It made me mad and I hit him. This teacher was back of me and he come down and he grabbed me right by the shirt collar and I had that necktie on and he twisted and yanked me right out of the seat. Well, I couldn't breathe. But I was big and rugged and nobody was going to take my breath away so I punched him two or three good ones right in the stomach and he let go.

And he said, "You're expelled! You're expelled! You can't go to school here again."

I went home and told my father. I'd taken that shirt off and Mother said, "What's that red streak around your neck?"

I said, "That's where that teacher choked me, I guess." I went and looked in the mirror and it was all red around there.

Dad looked at that. He said, "He done that?"

I said, "Yes."

"Well," he said, "if anybody put a mark like that on me, I'd put one on him." He says, "You go up there and you meet that teacher. You either give him a licking or you get one when you come home. This is your doings, you handle it yourself."

I went up to the old covered bridge. It was in the winter and it was dark. They used to hang the kerosene lanterns in the bridge. I hid in behind the girders of the bridge and I see him coming. I felt foolish and small about it afterwards, but I went out and told him, I says, "You take your coat and glasses off. I want to see if you're as good a man here as you were in school."

"Oh now, Azel, let's forget that, let's forget that."

I says, "I can't forget it. Take them glasses off."

He reached up and took his glasses off and he was taking his coat off. I laced into him.

I went home and I told Father what I done.

Father says, "Got any money?"

I says, "No."

He says, "Here's two dollars. I think you'll have to

The Covered Bridge. The Forks, Maine.

pay a dollar. Go right down to Judge Alkins there in Bingham, report it and pay for it."

I did.

Just about the time I was coming out of Judge Alkins', the head of the school board, Eddie Comber, and the teacher came down. Eddie Comber said, "We've got to put this boy under arrest."

Alkins said, "What for?"

He told him. Alkins said, "Now if you want to bring suit, you can bring suit. But there is no need to arrest."

So I come home and the school board and the town authorities decided to handle it all. I could go back to school, but I made up my mind I wouldn't, not while that teacher was there.

In just about a month's time he'd had trouble with somebody else and the school board decided to get rid of him. So I went back to school the next year.

I was a little late graduating. My wife and I started in the same year but I ended up graduating a year after she did.

The town of The Forks was a place in my days where that a major disaster could happen and it would never be known to the rest of the world. It was so far away and so quiet and everything.

But we used to have good times. The town of The Forks and West Forks had some darn good baseball players. Ever after I had them fingers cut off I never could handle a glove. So I started using a mitt and I'd catch. I recall one year when we played up in Jackman. It was the fourth of July and they wanted a double-header. Play Jackman, and the winner of The Forks and Jackman would play St. George.

So we went up there. I was catching. This Henry Pierce that usually caught for us was sick. Milton Morris, a second or third cousin of mine, he was pitching, with another fellow, Stanley Martin. But here I was doing all the catching. Oh, Stanley Martin had awful speed. He could throw that ball! We'd won that first game and my hand was all puffed right up, where it was pounded so much by the ball.

So I complained. We was eating dinner, and we was going to have to play St. George in the afternoon. I said, "No way am I going to be able to catch."

My cousin said, "Oh, we'll fix that."

He went to the back and he got a piece of steak from the kitchen, raw steak, and he said, "We'll fix that up."

He got ahold of some bicycle tape. They put that piece of steak right on my hand and then put tape around to hold it and I put my glove on and I caught nine more innings and we beat St. George. We had a punch bowl out in center field. We didn't dare to leave it in near home plate, there'd be too many into it. So they brought this big bucket of punch, plenty of alcohol in it, every now and then you go out to center field and get a drink.

This fellow, Milton Morris, when he died a few years ago we went to his funeral. I was a pallbearer. There was men there that I hadn't seen for forty years. One fellow spoke up and he says, "You know, boys," we was all off in the back room, "the whole Forks baseball team is here."

The pitcher was the guy who died.

When I was growing up at home there was always Saturday night entertainment somewhere. Either at the old Dwyer Hall or at the Bill Bowers' Hall at West Forks, or down at the Sterling Hotel in Caratunk. Any holiday, Christmas, Thanksgiving, it was always an occasion. It was either a barn dance or a box social. It is eight miles from The Forks to Caratunk, so if the dance were there somebody would have a pair of horses and a sleigh in the wintertime and we'd all go together. We'd go get there early and put the horses in the barn. We'd bring our soapstones into the hotel and put them on the old woodstove or in the oven. When we got ready to go, twelve or one o'clock in the morning, we'd grab the stones and put them on the floor of the sleigh and put our feet on them and wrap up in buffalo robes and head for home.

We used to have a pair of horses. One was a kicker. You'd just go to put a harness on her and she'd start kicking. Or you'd unbuckle a harness and just get it loose, you didn't have to take it off, she'd kick it off. Everybody was scared of her. Well, I got her harnessed and I went to a dance down in Caratunk one night. And I got introduced to a little bit of home-brew and I come home and oh was I tight. Singing and laughing. I unhitched the horse, put her in the barn and took care of the harness and went in to bed.

The next morning Mother said, "You was kind of happy when you come home last night."

"Oh," I said, "the dance hadn't all quit out of me yet."

She said, "How's it happen old Nellie didn't kick you when you fell right down behind her feet there?"

Father spoke up. He said, "A horse is pretty intelligent. It'll never kick a drunk or a fool."

That wasn't the first time I had been introduced to home-brew or cider. Young fellow, a friend of mine up at Durgin Corner was a Durgin boy. Well, there was a couple of girls that lived right there too, and their father and mother had gone to Skowhegan and they was going to stay overnight. We knew it, we was about fourteen, I guess. We got down there raising the devil, running around through the house and everywhere and some-body landed down cellar.

"Don't tip Father's cider over!"

So we decided we wanted some cider. The two girls got some dippers and come down and we drew off some cider and we started drinking. And we drank and drank and I didn't know any better. I was right in that cellar when my mother come to find me, get me to go home. Sick, I never was so sick in all my life as I was on that cider. My head, I thought it was going to bust. Every time my heart beat I'd feel it.

There was always little hoe-downs going at home and different places on Saturday night. My father could step dance and play the harmonica. My sister could step dance, the one next to me, oh, she was a wonderful step dancer. Most all of them could carry a tune, but I never could. All my music was in my feet. I never could sing or play the harmonica. There wasn't too many activities but dancing, so I had to learn how to dance.

I worked on the state road a lot and I went up to Jackman and I roomed out in town there off and on for two or three years. That was a playground for me because if I went out with anybody down at The Forks it would either be a cousin or a sister or somebody. I had to get out of town to get somebody that wasn't a relative of mine. So I went to a dance.

Of course I used to imbibe a little bit then. This one time I was feeling pretty good when I went to the dance and I got my eye on Marguerite. I danced with her once and I said, "How about going out, intermission, out to lunch?"

She said, "That all depends on what kind of condition you're in at intermission."

That kind of hit me, and I said to myself, "Well, if you're going to take her out you're going to quit drinking."

So I didn't drink any more and come intermission I took her out, her and her sister and a fellow that was playing in the orchestra.

They used to have contests in those days, waltzes, ballroom dancing, and the polka. That was my favorite. When you'd have a hundred couples competing for the best dancers and you end up on the floor with her and her sister, four of you, you know you had to be able to dance. We was two of the lightest people on our feet on the dance floor and there were some beautiful dancers in Jackman, Maine. There's Irish boys and Canadian men and the girls...But that night her sister beat us out.

There used to be a dance hall where Webb's Store is now in The Forks. Bill Bowers built a big dance hall there. When I was a young fellow, courting, she used to come down. There was a taxi, a seven-passenger Cadillac. It was thirty miles from Jackman to The Forks and the owner used to charge five dollars for that Cadillac for the evening. So five or six of them would get into the Cadillac and one of the boys would drive it. They'd come down to the dance. I used to be setting there waiting for them. I had a lot of competition. She liked to dance with a lot of different people.

There was always plenty of ways of getting alcohol, even in Prohibition. A friend and I, we made home-brew one summer in the woods, but we didn't cover it with cheese cloth, we just started it to work. 'Course these fly hatches come out. The only time we'd tend our home-brew or look at it was at night. This was Prohibition, and we didn't dare do any different. So when we thought the brew was ready, we took a capper, bottles, and everything and we went up there in the dark and started capping. We filled all these bottles and we carried them down to the road and hid them.

We drove to Jackman to go to a dance this one night; we took about half a case of that home-brew with us. Well, we took Marguerite and his girl friend and we went out at intermission and he and I, we wanted to drink the home-brew. All right, we pulled off and stopped off right in the churchyard where she goes to church. There was a street light there. I held one of them bottles up like that.

She says, "What are them, flies in there?"

That bottle was flies about three inches down. And he and I had been drinking it before.

You know, there used to be a fence between the Marshall Hotel and our old house up at the farm, and the young fellow who lived next door, he and I we watched a bootlegger. We was up above, on that ledge, above the hotel, and we see a great big car with a load of 'ban in it. He had stopped and we watched him take great big boxes of liquor and hide them down in the culvert. He drove off. Well this was supposed to be delivered for somebody to pick up, I guess. The young fellow and I went down and we took every bit of it and carried it into the woods. Well, these people at the hotel, sports, always wanted to buy a bottle of liquor, and so we were selling it five dollars a bottle. And you know where we'd hid it so no one would see it? At night we went over and pulled those fence posts up and put the bottle in the hole and put the post back down.

One day Mr. Marshall says to me, he says, "You and Pat (that's another fellow who worked for him) gotta go out and drive them posts in."

Come damn near making us do it that day. I went out and told my buddy about it and that night we pulled them posts and got all of our liquor out.

That was how we started bootlegging.

I had a still up in Jackman. I left it, it wasn't worth much. Bernard Berry, I, and Willy Dyer had it. We was hunting for Kaufman, the owner of Converse Shoes that had disappeared, and that's when we met this Willy Dyer. We helped him get that still in there. It was by a brook, under a ledge.

We carried grain in there - Bernard Berry was the one who carried the grain. He was a uncle of mine, almost my age. We'd mix it up, sugar and grain and water, and cover the barrels with cheese cloth. Then after it would get done we'd fill the still up and set a fire. But we'd burn at night when nobody was around. We only fired her up a few times but we'd had to fire her up on dark, dark nights.

About eight, ten years ago I was up there in that area hunting. It was always good bird-hunting there and I followed that brook down. The timber companies had cut in the area but most of the still was there.

About that same time, Mother and Father was running the sporting camps over at Otter Pond and I was bell-hopping at Marshall's and I used to guide on the Kennebec. Well, the sports was always looking for liquor. I had an old 1924 Chevrolet touring car with no top on it or anything. I run it around a lot and it couldn't go too fast and I wasn't proud of it, but my father had a Nash Advance Six. You could reel the windows up. The top was something like a touring car. Seven passenger. Every now and then I'd get that; Father'd want me to do an errand or something. Sometimes he'd want me to take a message to this bootlegger in Jackman. The bootlegger was to bring the liquor down and Father would have somebody out on the road at a certain place. When I would tell him, or if I called him up I'd tell him that my father wanted two guides, or he wanted a couple of waitresses. Well, that either meant Scotch or whiskey.

This time I told my father I had tried to call but I couldn't get him.

Father says, "You go up and see him. You be sure and tell him."

Well, I drove to Jackman. I told him what my father wanted. I knew he was a bootlegger. I said ,"How much does that whiskey cost?"

"Three dollars a bottle."

When he used to deliver it down to The Forks, I knew

because Father had given me money to give to him, it was seven dollars a bottle. So my uncle, Bernard Berry, and I, we loaded up the car. We come down to The Forks and we hid the stuff there.

We was telling some of the sports and some of the people in the dancehall that we knew where we could get a bottle from somebody.

"How much it cost?"

"Seven dollars."

They'd give us seven dollars, we'd take off and get them a bottle. We done that time and again.

One time I recall. Mother and Father were out of camp and staying at home in The Forks. I got the old Hudson - we had a Hudson then- and my uncle and I went to Jackman and got a case of whiskey and two bags of beer. That Canadian beer used to come in burlap bags wrapped in paper. You'd buy that beer for a dollar a bottle. We were almost back to The Forks and coming down Durgin Hill. We come around a turn and here was car lights facing right at us, two men out in the road waving to stop us. I looked and one was Elmer Adams, the high sheriff of Somerset County, the other guy was the local sheriff from Bingham. I wasn't about to stop and weaved by them and as I drove by them I could see one of them shooting at the tire.

They was headed the wrong way and we were going, we had momentum up. We got down to my mother's place, went around back to the barn, dug a hole in the wood pile, grabbed the whiskey and beer, covered it up, run the old car to one side and went in the house.

Bernard says, "I'm not going in. I'm going home."

He had to walk two miles to get home.

I went in the kitchen door. Mother's bedroom was right by the porch.

Car drove into the yard. Two men got out and come onto the porch, pounded on the door.

Father jumped up, says, "What do you want?"

The sheriff says, "Your car just come in?"

Father says, "You here, Azel?"

I says, "Yes, I just come in."

They come right through into the kitchen, lit a lamp. The sheriff says, "Why didn't you stop?"

I says, "I didn't know who it was, whether it was a holdup or what." I started walking right by him.

"Hold on here, young fellow."

Father said, "Come back here. What's going on?"

I says, "I was coming down Durgin Hill and car lights right into my face and as I go by here's two plainclothesmen out in the road with guns. I'm not going to stop for that."

Father says, "You weren't in uniform, you fellows?"

"No."

"Well, I don't blame you, Son."

I'm telling you I was awful glad when Father and Mother left that next morning for camp and I could peek at that wood pile and get that stuff out.

I want to say a little more about my grandfather. My grandfather on my mother's side was of a family of thirteen children and he was a blacksmith. Father's side, he had three uncles who was blacksmiths, but I always liked my grandfather and had a lot of respect for him. He could do anything. He could fix your watch or he'd cut your hair or he would shoe your horse. He made axes in an ax factory in Caratunk for years, but that was before I was born.

Mr. Holway run the local store. He practically governed the town, low key, helping everybody. He had a lot of big tables. He used to pile men's pants and men's clothing and everything on them. He wanted a rail put on the tables to keep stuff from sliding off. So he got my grandfather to come down. Why I remember this, I was with my grandfather at the time. I was probably twelve, thirteen years old. We went into the store and took all the measurements of the tables.

Grandfather says, "By Geez, young fella, you and I got to go to work."

A lot of times I was his third hand around the shop. I recall him welding those rails and explaining to me just how it worked.

My grandfather was the only man that I ever see that, in an open forge, a blacksmith's forge, could take and braze and weld two pieces of steel together. When he done it he used the brass offen the bottom of a light bulb. You break a light bulb and you cut that end off and you pound it out flat and you have pieces of brass. He'd have his two pieces of iron white-hot and he'd put the brazing compound on there and he'd drop that piece of brass in between the two pieces of iron and pound them just to stick them together. Put them back in the fire and reheat them right to a braze.

He says, "By God, I don't know there's another damn fool in the country that's ever tried this."

Well, I was just as proud, every time I'd go in that grocery store and I'd see people looking at the rails. "What's that brass in there, that brazing?"

"Yes," Mr. Holway'd say, "We have a very clever man in town. He brazed that. It has been quite a conversation piece."

In later years, it was after I was married, I looked at that rail and I said to the people run the store, "Boy, I'd like to have that when you're done with it."

"You can have it. You're welcome to it." But I never got it.

When I was about fifteen, sixteen years old, I had a little horse and I called her Susie, a little mare horse. Come wintertime and ice and snow and everything, it wasn't safe for her to be out so I called my grandfather up and I asked him if he would shoe my horse.

"No, hellity damn, of course I ain't going to shoe your horse for you," he says.

So I was ready to hang up. I felt kind of bad.

But he said, "If I was a boy and owned a horse, I think I'd learn how to shoe it myself."

"But Grampa, I haven't got any shoes."

"Hellity Jesus," he says, "get up here and make 'em."

"I don't know how."

"Well, I always showed you how, didn't I?" This was my grandfather Berry.

So come Saturday I called him and I said, "If I can get that horse up there... you think I should walk her up?"

"Walk right along the side of the road," he said, "where it's gravel and don't ride her and she'll come up here and not hurt herself."

So I did. I left early in the morning and I got up there around eight o'clock.

"Well," he said. "might as well put her in the barn."

He says, "You know the size of the shoe she wears."

I said, "I don't know."

"Well, gol darn it, find out!"

He led the horse into the blacksmith shop, picked up her foot and showed me how to measure it, for the size and everything. And after he done that he said, "Put her down in the barn, feed her."

I put her down.

He had two forges there, he was using one. "Stoke that forge up."

I stoked it up.

The shoes weren't bent or nothing, they was straight pieces of iron. So he pulled a piece of iron out.

"Now," he says, "you measure that and mark it with the cold chisel, every length you're going to cut off. Then you put that cold cut on that anvil and you use a four-pound hammer and you cut 'em off."

I did. Got them all cut off.

He was making a set of shoes and he said, "Now you watch me, and do what I do." He says, "You get them hot and you bend 'em, shape 'em."

He had a big iron horn out there, an anvil they called

it, out there on the floor, and it had gauges set for different circles. You take hold of the shoe in the middle and you put it on the anvil and you pound the iron bar until you bend it and fit it.

Well, I worked all the forenoon just getting them four pieces of iron cut and bent. We went to dinner.

"Now," he says, "you know what you got to do."

I says, "I don't know what I got to do."

"Well," he says, "you put the groove for the nails. And then you got to punch the nail holes through."

I says, "All right," and we started.

And then you had to bend the heel cocks, sharpen them, and the last thing was to weld the toe cock on.

"Now," he says, "I'm going to stand right by you and watch you." And he did.

About eight o'clock at night I had finished making four shoes.

"There, by God, young fella, ain't that lot better pair of shoes than I could make?" He says, "You done it yourself. Learn to do something yourself always. Well, we better call it a day. In the morning we'll bring the horse up here and we'll shoe her."

Next morning I brought her up, got all the shoeing tools out. He showed me how to cut down the horse's hoof and fit the shoe to it. When I got it all fitted, "There," he says, "now you can nail them on."

This is the thing that I was scared of, driving the nail, might drive it into the horse's foot.

He showed me how to hold the hoof, hold the shoe on and everything, put the nail in...That nail is built so it's slanted on one end to make it steer out instead of going into the hoof.

He said, "Now don't make a mistake and get that going the wrong way or if you do you're apt to pick yourself up from over in the corner if you hurt that little horse."

"OK." I shod that horse and when I got done, I guess around ten, eleven o'clock, I got onto her back and rode home and I was a pretty proud boy.

The things that he could do, and I had a lot of uncles and they could do about everything. This was the way they brought us up, trained us.

There was a bunch of fellows used to come up fishing and hunting. They came from Portland. I recall one time they came with a Model T Ford and they was up above Johnson Mountain in a camp. When they started home they broke an X in this Ford. That was the axle, but we used to call it the X. My uncle, he was a year older than I was, he and I took the old Reo truck and we went and towed them into my grandfather's garage. We got into the garage, jacked the car up and took out the X. This was Saturday afternoon. The only place that might have a new X was Skowhegan and that was forty-five miles away. Everything in Skowhegan was closed anyway.

"Well, I guess you fellows will have to be satisfied with staying here."

"We got to be at work Monday morning."

We was debating whether my uncle would take the Reo truck and haul them clear down to Portland, some hundred and forty miles. They had some whiskey and they was giving my grandfather a little bit, talking.

One of them says, "Tom, you can put that together. Damn it all, you can weld that."

Grandfather looked at the X and says, "By God, we'll give it a try."

My grandfather made a new fire, everything had to be clean. He heated the forge up. He took a piece of angle iron and laid it on the anvil and measured the right length....Anyway he welded the pieces together to make a new X.

"There," he says to my uncle and me. "Put the car together."

Now, this is amusing because on the rear end of the old Model T Ford the ring gear went around and the drive shaft came down with a gear that drove the ring gear. When it was on the left-hand side it was right. But if the ring gear were on the right-hand side it would be turned over and it would be wrong. When you put the car in low gear you'd be in reverse. So my uncle and I weren't paying attention, doing it fast and everything, putting it back together. The men got in the car, four of them, I can see them now, ready to go. They went to put it into reverse to come out of the garage and they was going ahead. They all laughed.

My grandfather said, "You eagles (that's what he called us), you've let me down. I told them in an hour's time they'd be going."

It took us just about an hour to take the car apart, turn that gear over and put it back together. By that time they'd drank quite a bit more of that bottle. When those fellows headed out they was pretty happy.

My grandfather says to my uncle and me, "You fellows better not go taking off anywhere. I think you'll be called to haul them back."

The next spring those fellows came back and they had two X's in the back seat of the car. But they still had the one that my grandfather had jumped together.

I remember one winter my father was making skis for all of us kids. My brother Clyde was exceptionally good. He'd go up on the mountain before it was all growed up and he'd get on one ski and come down. He'd go clear to the river. Oh, he had good balance.

We used to cut an ash and split it. We'd get it about an inch, two inch thick, a straight ash. We'd put it on the wood vise and we'd drawknife it out and shape it and get it where we'd want. We used to put a strap right straight through the ski for the toe and that one strap was the only thing we had to hold our boots on the ski. We never had a harness until late years. We'd make the skis narrow for cross-country. We'd make them about, some were ten foot long. When we would turn them up we'd just take a round log laying down, put another one close to it, and take the ends of the skis and put them in boiling water for a good hour, two hours, until they were good and hot. Then we'd stick them in between the logs and bend them down over and weight them. Leave them until they were dry. Then when they got all dried out we would put the linseed oil to them, and that would keep the water from going in and straightening the ski back out.

We made toboggans for trapping. Dad made one of them. He laminated the wood so that at the place the toboggan started to bend it narrowed right in and then curled right back. It was tied down to a board across. He had one eye bolt in there and the dogs used to haul by that. They come hit a tree or anything and the toboggan would just go around. The tobaggon was probably six or seven feet long. We put an oilcloth in it; it was tied to the slats. Anything you put on the sled you folded the cloth up over it and tied it. You never lost anything that way.

It was hard to make friends with any wild animal. Back in those days they had no chain saws. They didn't have the automobile roads. A deer today will hide behind a little fir bush and let you walk right by him, because he has seen so many tractors go by and so many people and automobiles that it just don't pay to run. Back in those days for a man to get a deer he had to be a fairly good hunter. He had to stalk the deer. And you had to be quiet. You had to work the downwind side of the animal.

We used to have a spruce partridge. We have them now, but they aren't like they used to be. They've been killed off and interbred and everything. But the old spruce partridge was almost all black and a dark dark green in it. Red on the side of his head. He would very seldom fly, he'd just hop up on the limb of a tree or something. They were well protected in those days, that and the porcupine, because they said if a person got lost or anything they could throw a rock and kill a spruce partridge or they could run down a porcupine and have something to eat.

When I was a kid, twelve, thirteen years old, that was the respect we had. When I became about sixteen the lumber companies decided that the porcupine was doing damage to the wood lots so they put a twenty-five cent bounty for each porcupine. A kid wanted a quarter for a haircut or something he 'd find himself a porcupine.

Well, there was five or six of us boys who were porcupine hunters and we used go up to the old fellow who was the town clerk who used to give us a quarter, but we had to take four feet of the porcupine with us. The clerk owned a farm and at night somebody would bring in probably three or four sets of porcupine feet and the clerk would throw them in a bucket. When he'd go out to milk his cows he'd take them out and throw them out the window into the manure pile. Some of the kids playing around there see him and told the other ones. So the kids started picking up them porcupine feet, taking them home and bringing them back up to the clerk and getting a quarter. They figured they got about four dollars off of one porcupine.

My father was the caretaker and guide for the Otter Pond Camps and in the mid-twenties he spent much of his time there. The camps are across and down the Kennebec River from The Forks.

When I was about my third year in high school I used to go down to Otter Pond Landing on the Kennebec to pick up my dad. He'd be coming out from camp, home for overnight or something and I'd meet him in the evening and then take him back to the landing in the morning. After he crossed the river he had two miles and a half to walk in. Well, this evening I went down, I went early. I got out of school about around three thirty. He was going to be down at the river around five. I parked the car right there where the crossing place was and I went up on the side hill where there used to be an old farm. I went up there and I sit down on a log for a while and the sun was shining and first thing I know I looked and a little deer poked his head and looked at me. Had little horns about that long.

"Well," I said, "that ought to be good eating."

So I shot him, dressed him off. Dragged him down and put him on the running board of the old car. Waited for Dad to come. He didn't look the deer over too much. He got in the car and we went home. My sister and I took the deer and hung it up in the barn. My father went out the next day and he was looking the deer over and he come back in. He said, "You know you have a freak out there?"

I said, "What do you mean?"

He said, "That deer has got six legs."

We laughed and I says, "Oh no it hasn't."

He says, "Well, you go out and look."

We went out and looked, and it had a little foot coming out the back of both front legs and there was an extra bone, but it was under the skin from the knee down, and then this little foot hung out in back.

I've asked biologists and they said that they never knew of any cases like that since, so it really was not too common.

The odd part of it was that another time when I was hunting I shot I think the mother of that deer. It was right on a sharp side hill and there was a ledge below with a steep drop off. The deer was feeding along the edge of the ledge. It was bright sun and I see the outline of this doe feeding in the oak. So I pulled up and shot it. The deer ran down hill, took right off and it jumped out over the ledge. There was a cluster of about four maple trees all together growing below that ledge and that deer jumped right up into the top of those trees. There she was. I looked at it, it was getting late, time for my father to be coming so I went down to the car. He was there waiting for me.

He said, "What are you doing? I heard you shoot."

I said, "I shot a deer."

He says, "Where is it?"

"It's up a tree. I can't get it down."

We had to cut one of them six-inch maples in order to get the deer out of that tree and get it down to dress it off.

About 1930, my father and my uncle were beaver trapping in on the Enchanted Township, and they built a camp place there near a ledge on the brook. Probably it was an open affair. They had fires against the ledge to reflect the heat back into the lean-to, and my dad said that a big chunk of that rock popped off in the heat. They looked at it and they could see this white fiber in there. They brought a piece of that rock out and they knew it was asbestos and everybody see it was asbestos. Well, they went and told the people that owned the land that they had found some asbestos. The owners wanted to know where it was and my father and uncle said for a fee they would tell them. They wanted two thousand dollars.

The land owners wouldn't pay it. But they contacted Johns-Manville. Johns-Manville right off contacted some mineralogists and sent them in to the woods. They hired a cook and these three men. I hauled them in with a team and my uncle was doing their cooking. It wasn't long before we got a call and they wanted two more men to come to work in there. So my uncle who was about my age and brother to the one that was doing the cooking and I went in for three dollars for a night and half a day. They wanted us to pack the rock back to the base camp. We went in and started work. They tried time and again to find out from me where this asbestos was because they found out that my father was the one who had found the mine.

So when I come home I told my father, "They think I ought to know where that asbestos is."

He says, "Where are they working?"

I told him.

"Well," he says, "they're way off."

So after the Johns-Manville people were done and my father wasn't well and not expected to live he told me right where to find it. My brother Oliver knows. I've been there. Of course asbestos has no value at all now.

The one big forest fire that I recall, I recall all of them, but the one big one that really burnt a lot of timber and land was the Indian Pond fire. Indian Pond Township, Dead Stream, Chase Stream, all burned at once, three or four townships. This was 1931 or 32. The railroad had stopped service from Bingham to Somerset Junction up at Rockwood, but the tracks was still there.

Anyway, this fire started back of Indian Pond. I daresay the fire had been burning a week or ten days before I got up there. They took a train load of us up - just a flat car with a bunch of men on it. They took a lot of blankets for the men that was already up there. They had maybe five hundred men up there fighting fire. We was down south going up the railroad track and what wind there was was bringing the smoke down to us. Everybody was coughing, sneezing. We went through fire on both sides of the railroad tracks. We could hardly breathe.

They got us into Indian Pond. Right away they said they wanted the pumps over across the dam pumping water. The fire was back in there a half, three-quarters of a mile. They set up two pumps right there at the dam.

The fire warden said to me, "You can run those, can't you?"

I said, "Oh yes."

He left me with a few cans of gasoline mixed for the pumps. He says, "You give us a half hour."

A crew of men were laying hoses back into the woods and they were carrying a barrel and some more pumps, so they could relay the water. Everything was dry. They hadn't had any rain for two, three months.

So I set there. Pumped all night. Some fellows would come out and say, "We've got it down. We have it licked..." through the night. "Keep the water going."

I thought I was doing a good job.

About ten o'clock the next day they brought in another pump for me and they run a line into the woods. They carried more barrels and more pumps into the woods. About two o'clock in the afternoon these people begun to come out of there. Just before sundown that night the wind was blowing and that fire was coming through toward us. I can see it now. I'd have given anything to have been able to have a picture. I see men, deer and bear all go into that lake ahead of that fire. Swallows would be flying around there, circling, and you'd see them drop.

That fire, when it jumped Indian Pond at that point, just above the dam, was blazing three or four hundred feet into the air, lapping up over us. Nobody got burnt or caught in it, I don't know why. But I know a lot of men ran in front of that fire when the wind come up and they was jumping into the lake. It eventually burnt clear through to Dead Stream.

I stayed on the fire another two weeks. I come out of there August 8th. It was my birthday and I'd been in there a couple of weeks so they let me out. I happened to be in town four or five days afterwards and the chief fire warden, his name was Ralph Sterling, wanted to know if I would patrol days from Ellis Pond to Indian Pond. Nine miles one way. The fire had burnt right up close to Ellis Pond. The fire wasn't out, it was burning here and there underground. I got two dollars and fifty cents a day. They allowed me a dollar a day for board. So I walked eighteen miles a day, seven days a week.

It was set up to keep me honest. There was a fire phone at Dead Stream and there was another one at Indian Pond, and another at Ellis Pond. So I would get up in the morning and I would travel over to Dead Stream. I would report in on the fire line, then I'd go on to Indian Pond and call in on that line. Then I'd come back at night and call in from Ellis Pond. Seven days a week. But boy, didn't I enjoy it. All I had to do was just walk and enjoy the woods and I always had my little telescope fishrod with me. All of them little streams and brooks had trout in them and I'd catch enough to eat and I'd eat trout three times a day. Pancakes and trout.

I stayed there about three weeks before we got a good big rain. That was in the fall of the year.

It was in February of the next year when I was trapping with my dad. We was in back of Horseshoe Pond. There was one other party of men, two brothers, the Cementbergs of Moxie, they were trapping too. We was going up this beaver bog, walking along, Dad said to me, "I can smell smoke. It must be the Cementbergs are camping somewhere."

I said, "Do you think they would be camping up in here?"

He said, "Well, I can smell wood smoke, can't you?" I said, "Yes, I can."

We travelled a little bit further, and going by the way the wind come Dad said, "Let's go up in there and see if they're camped up there."

We go up and have a look. It was a peat bog. We had four feet of snow in the woods that we was snowshoeing through but we come into this peat bog that was all afire. You could walk right along the edge of that peat bog and it was sheer cut. All that snow come but the peat just kept burning. It looked like six feet deep that had burnt, and it covered about an acre.

So a fire can last a long time.

About the second or third year after that burn, there was one hell of a blueberry industry there. There was people coming from down on the coast and everywhere and they went into the burn to rake the berries. They had horses and wagons hauling the berries out to the rail-head. I think they even run special trains up there to get the berries out. Oh, there was a thousand people there, and, boy, they were beautiful big blueberries. When anything like that happens there is always some good comes of it.

Sometimes I would haul men from the railhead at Moxie to go to work on the Enchanted. I had seats on the long sled and I had two horses. In those days I'd get a dollar and a quarter per person for hauling those people from the railhead into the lumber camp. Well, six of them, that was a good day's pay.

I'd go into Moxie and I'd put the horses in the barn and let them rest, feed them. When the train come at one thirty, two o'clock, I'd get hitched on and go. We'd go in from up top of Durgin Hill just above The Forks and go in on the Enchanted toward Dead River. I went to Enchanted Number Two camp, they called it, in there about eight miles from the road. It was about eight more miles to the railhead from home so by the time I dropped the men off I'd gone about twenty-four miles. So when I'd get in to the lumber camp I'd feed the horses and I'd eat supper, then I'd come out and I'd have just a lantern hanging by me on the sled. This one time we was trotting along and I come across a bog. Well these horses had gone quite a ways and we was trotting to get across that bog and going towards home. The light from that lantern was just enough to create light on them phosphorous gases going up. Big balls of light. The horses spied them. They took off. I couldn't have held them if I wanted to. I think I was just a scaret as the horses. I didn't know what it was.

Well, I come out and I told my father about it and he says, "What did you have for supper tonight?"

He thought a while. Then he said, "It could be gases coming out of the peat bog. If you hadn't of had the light it wouldn't have shined and you wouldn't have seen it."

You can see them on a moonlit night too.

The S.D. Warren Paper Co. was logging then back in on the Enchanted. That was a big area there. The men was cutting popple a lot, peeling it. They'd cut and peel in the

Creative Survival

summer, then in the fall they'd saw it up and in the winter they'd haul it out.

My sister next to the oldest one, her husband was a logging foreman. They had thirty-five or forty Frenchmen there in the woods, cutting pulp. They was living in a tarpaper camp where they was logging. This bear was getting into the dingle, the shed where they kept the food and the molasses and stuff, and they had to get rid of him. I was home, working there at Marshall's and my sister'd called my dad. She wanted my father to come get the bear.

He said, "Why don't you shoot him?"

"Well, we've tried to watch for him but we aren't getting him. He always comes when we aren't seeing him."

Father says, "You get hold of Azel and have him go in with the traps."

I had to go way in to Otter Pond and get two traps. The next day I went in to the Enchanted. It was on a Thursday. I got into camp about dark so I didn't do anything about the bear.

Well, the blacksmith they had in the camp there, and the filer, they took a twenty-gallon molasses barrel, took the top hoop off, took the head out. They sharpened twenty penny spikes needle-sharp and they drove them in on a slant right straight around, and then they put that hoop back on. They put some molasses in the bottom of the barrel and a loaf of bread.

That night in the camp we heard a noise. A bunch of us got up - we was in our underwear and everything. We had two flashlights shining. Here this bear was, setting on his haunches and roaring and hollering, trying to get that barrel off. He couldn't get his head out of that barrel. Well, the cookee, his name was Marshall O'Neil, he was a hellion anyway, he had a twenty-two rifle. He got right down behind me and he shot between my legs into that bear, and that bear took off. Well, the men's camp had two rows of bunks in that tarpaper shack. It was just a few boards and strapping and poles. The doors was screen doors to keep the flies out. That bear went right straight through, right in and over them fellows in the bunk and out the other side, down into the woods, hollering. Them Frenchmen was up all night. The next morning they all quit. My brother-in-law, wasn't he wild!

You know, that bear never came back.

Creative Survival

CHAPTER THREE

Guiding (1928-1932)

I guided before I got out of high school. After I got into that little altercation with the principal and I left high school for about a year.... These guiding jobs, they weren't steady. They might go for two days, they might go for a week. The sports might fish from the Marshall House on the river for two or three days and then they might go into Ellis Pond or Pierce Pond. I think guiding's one of the worst jobs. When I was guiding I was taught by my father and other guides. We had to furnish all of the dishes, we had to furnish the blankets, the bedding, and it would have to be clean every time we'd go out. We'd have to have either a tent or know where there was a lean-to we could get into. Everything had to be planned. You'd cook all your meals. You didn't carry a loaf of bread in the woods, it was most always fish chowder or broiled fish. That L. L. Bean wire broiler that they'd sell back in those days, every guide had one or two of them. You get a nice trout or togue or salmon you split them right open and lay them between that, put them over the hot coals, you get the smoke taste. There's nothing any better in my mind than a trout broiled by the camp fire. You can have all the fry pans you want.

I guided in to Otter Pond Camps because when you guide in a camp like that you don't do any cooking out unless you go on a picnic. But to cook breakfast, dinner and supper and set up camp I just thought was too much. I stayed away from the Allagash trip after a couple of times. That was a lot of work. Paddle, carry canoes, carry the food, paddle all day long. The last trip I'll never forget. It was with Mr. and Mrs. Webster. He was the cartoonist for Andy Gump. She was writing all the time and she didn't paddle. But he was paddling with my buddy. It was work then.

Back when I was guiding at the Marshall Hotel we used to pole twenty-foot canoes, and we'd pole them up the Kennebec about a mile above Stand Up Rips, and sometimes the people we were guiding would walk up the trail. The timber companies would be sluicing logs at high water, but we'd go up on the high water rather than the low water because you'd stay near the shores and the current wasn't so great in on the shore as it was out in the middle. As the water'd get low, it would be concentrated and rough and hard going out in the middle, and you couldn't go out on the shores. You always pole up on the high water. A sixteen-foot pole, and we'd have our paddles in the canoe. Our poles was double ended, iron on one end and wood on the other. So we'd use our iron pole till we got up the river to Elm

Tree Campground.

The sports would walk in, and we'd cook the dinner. About one, two o'clock we'd get in the canoes and we'd start dropping down the river. Well, I used the wood end of the pole then 'cause when you'd snub the canoe, you know, you wouldn't spook the fish. The iron would spook the fish.

In those days about every rock, big boulder out in the middle of the stream, might hold a fish. You stop the canoe quite a little ways from that and let your fisherman drop his fly down and we used to tell them to get it right on the slick where the water'd start breaking to go around the rock, let the fly go down there. The salmon would always lay right above the rock right where it would break, but down under the rock if you let your fly go down there and sink with the current underneath of the back of the rock downstream you would pick up a trout. By the time we got about six or seven miles down there by The Forks they might have a couple, three salmon, trout.

The people that stayed at Marshall's were well-to-do people. Victor Lershner was president of the Bowery Savings Bank. I guided him, an awful nice man. Major Boyers and his wife, they always stayed two months every year. She'd employ me as a guide and she didn't like fishing. My father used to pole him on the river and he was always fly fishing. He had an artificial leg. But I was always having to take hikes with her, and she was writing books, and writing stories. She was always writing and all I had to do was pack her lunch and carry her lunch, make sure she didn't get lost and got back. That was the type of people that come there to the hotel at that time. They were moneyed people.

Board and room per person was twenty-five dollars a week and that included three meals a day, room with bath, and it was seventeen dollars a week for a kid under fifteen years of age.

I used to drawshave logs when I was a young fellow. That was my art. I remember Sam Allen and his brother-in-law, Charlie Crotto, was building some camps. They'd cut the logs and get them out of the woods and I'd drawshave them. I guess I got the knack and I had the drawknives that my father had had. You know, you peel a log and you try to put it into a camp just by peeling it on the sap line, it will turn black and look ugly. So what we always had to do was take the drawshaver and take that sap line out. That way they'd stay nice and white and turn gray evenly. So just about every log they had in them camps I had drawshaved. I learned how to notch corners, how to lay logs, how to build camps. Then I got out of that.

My father built camps before I can even remember. He built the Lang cottage near Parlin, and then we built the five camps back of the Parlin Hotel. Sandy Harris was with us. Those were big camps, two, three bed rooms in each log camp. It would take us three months or better to build one camp.

In 1938, I built two simple log camps, 18 by 14 with

porches on them. Five hundred dollars apiece. Built the sink, side boards all in, the tables, the bunks, built the whole camp, five hundred dollars. Done one of them in fifteen days. Four men and myself. Built them for an immigration officer and another man on Moose River. The camps are at Spencer Rips.

What I did, I had an old pulp truck and I went to Canada and I bought a horse and harness for twenty-five dollars. I had to have a horse to yard the wood out. Put him in the truck, put a frame up. Then I went and bought a bunch of matched boards for flooring and roof of the camps. About two thousand, three thousand board feet, and a few bunches of shingles.

Went up to Attean, unloaded the horse. One of the men that was working for me took the horse in on the old telephone line going into Spencer. The other men and I, we took two canoes and filled them with boards and shingles and everything, carried over the Attean Rips up into the Moose River and went up from there eight miles to Spencer Rips. We got all unloaded that night, the horse had got there and had been fed, and we were clearing a spot to build the camp. We built a lean-to for us to stay in, and it was fifteen days from the time we landed there till the time that the first camp was done.

The Otter Pond Camps are really the only camps that are one hundred percent out of the woods - no sawed lumber or anything. Even the window frames. Ed Gomery who owned the Hudson-Essex assembly factory there in Pennsylvania and Roberts who had the

Nash-LaFayette automobile bought the old camps. Father had guided them, and when they bought the camps they hired my father to be guide and caretaker. There were camps already at Otter Pond, but Mr. Gomery and Mr. Roberts wanted new ones.

We built two camps. The roofs was all cedar split. My father hired two brothers, Simon and Forest Cates, that was very clever with adzes, broad axes and things. There were three or four others, a pair of horses.

The floor in those camps was put down as poles. They'd lay the poles across, butt to top, butt to top. But they'd hew the sides so that they fit just as tight as a board. Then there was that round left. After they got the floor all laid, one of those fellows would start in one corner with an adz and he'd shave that all down and you could hardly see an adz mark on that floor. Ed Gormery wanted the camp built this way.

Then they went out into the woods and split out the cedar roofing boards, cedar splits we used to call them. They'd cut the log in three-foot lengths. They'd stand the log up and split it with a froe and a hammer. A froe is a knife with the handle mounted at right angles to the blade. Then you get a whole bunch of splits and you'd put them on a bench and drawknife them so that they would fit when they were laid on the roof. The purlins were about three feet apart and they'd nail the splits to them. And they were watertight. That was in 1925, 26.

After my father went to Otter Pond, he didn't have much to do with Ellis Pond Camp. He stayed at Otter

Pond. The Otter Pond people went in to Ellis some. They would call, and my mother and I would walk in and clean up the camps and sometimes we'd take the old horse and take in a bunch of groceries, and get in there and turn the horse loose and he'd go home. That was the Tennessee Walker. That horse could walk about six miles an hour. Head right down just a-going. I never cared much for the Otter Pond Camps, but I loved Ellis Pond.

My dad owned the Ellis Pond Camp before I was born. Mother and Father was married in 1906. My father and grandfather built this two story-and-a-half building with an ell on each side and a porch the full length of it. Most all built out of spruce and cedar, and it had a cedar split roof.

As a boy fifteen or sixteen years old I used to brag that I could go out on that lake anytime from ice out till it froze up in the fall, I'd get my twenty-five fish in an hour.

We used to smoke trout in at Ellis Pond. We used to take old steel barrels, cut the head out of each barrel, poke holes through the side of the barrel and use little three/eighths-round iron rods. Take the trout out of the salt brine, slide the rod in, put the fish on and keep sliding and when you get the rod full, slide the rod out the other side. Start another one. Fill that barrel with trout hanging in there. Build a a little fire, and you'd keep a lot of hardwood sawdust over it so that it's smoking, set the barrel over it with a wooden cover on it and smoke all day, eight to ten hours. We used to

Smoking Barrel.

smoke those trout for the sports to take out of there to take to New York, Philadelphia, wherever.

It was a simple thing and I think it was one of the better smoke systems that you can get. We had two rings on the barrel, that we could put a pole through and two of us could pick it up, set it off, and make sure our fire wasn't getting too hot. It worked nice.

I never knew of any pond in Maine that used to produce the fish that Ellis Pond did. In those days you were allowed twenty-five. But it was so far to walk there wasn't too many people fishing it. Then they started logging in there.

One time, it was in the 1920's, my father was managing the Otter Pond Club. The people that came to Otter Pond wanted to go to Ellis Pond for a week or two fishing in the 10,000 Acre area, which at that time was the best. Mother decided that the kitchen in the Ellis Pond camp had to have new cupboards, a counter and sink. She asked my grandfather who she could get to do the work. He asked her what she was paying.

"Five dollars a day."

He said, "I'll do it if Azel helps."

He said it would take two to three weeks, so as soon as school was out for the summer he and I went in. I don't think I had ever seen my grandfather so happy as the three weeks he was in there working.

About this time the fishing laws had changed to fly fishing only on Ellis, Horseshoe and Round Ponds, and the daily limit was reduced from twenty-five to fifteen fish. There was three or four fly rods hanging in camp.

I said, "Let's go get some fish for supper."

He took an old steel telescope rod.

I said, "You can't fly fish with that."

"I know it and I'm not going to."

You could always dig worms where the waste water from the sink came out. Well, he went out and got some worms and we went fishing. We got plenty for a couple of days. I was some nervous as I knew we would have more fishing to do and the game warden's camp was up to the head of the lake about a mile from our camp. It was the office camp of a previous logging job. The camp set back about a quarter mile from the pond.

We had been working on the kitchen about four days when Bob Moore, the game warden, his wife, his sister and brother-in-law paid us a visit. They wanted to use a couple boats to go fishing. The warden looked out the window and saw where Grandfather had dug some worms.

He said, "I hope you fellows aren't fishing with worms."

Grandfather said, "Do you think the fish are any better caught by flies than bait?"

He said, "I hope I don't have to issue either of you a summons."

When they got ready to leave Grandfather was down at the pond with us and the warden said, "Mr. Berry, I will be down some evening and I will paddle you so you can fly fish."

Grandfather said, "I hope you can swim. I get ner-

Creative Survival

vous in a canoe sometimes."

We went over to Island Pond one afternoon and I don't believe I have ever seen a prettier catch of trout as he caught. Fifteen fish, one to two pounds apiece.

We were on our way out and we met the warden. Grandfather showed him the fish. That evening the warden came down and had supper with us. Mother called and I told her about the fish Grandfather had caught at Island Pond and she said she and Grandmother would like a feed. We needed a few things and I told her if she could get them I would meet her at Cold Stream Depot Camps at 10 the next morning.

I was up about four and went fishing and got 15 more trout, ate breakfast and took Grandfather's fish and mine and hit the trail. I told Grandfather I should be back about three p.m.

After I left the warden came down and visited. He helped Grandfather for three or four hours and he got to calling him Tom, and Grandfather was calling him Bob. Around two p.m. Bob said, "Let's go up to Wilson Hill Pond." It was about one and a half miles from Ellis Pond.

Bob said, "I know where the boat is and you can bait-fish there."

They left a note for me and about six o'clock they came back laughing and happy. Bob finally got Grandfather to use flies and from that day on I don't think he ever bait fished again.

There was a very close relationship between him and Robert Moore. Bob would always find time to stop and say hello when he was in the neighborhood. I know I missed Bob when they transferred him. He was always ready to give me a hand or advice. And I grieved his sudden death. I lost a good friend.

My dad and I was trapping one winter in on Ten Thousand Acres, and about a mile, mile and a half from our Ellis Pond camp was this logging camp. So father says, "Let's stop in."

He knew the jobber there. He says, "I want to buy some bacon or meat - some food for us."

He went in and he was told to go down and see the cook. So we went down and went into the cook camp. The men's camp is on this end and then what they call the dingle, in between, and then the cook camp. Well I stopped at the dingle and looked and there was a box about six foot square. Had a cover that come down over it to keep the animals out. But the cover was open and it had a good foot of trout just about twelve inches long. They had been out ice fishing in that pond and supplying the men.

The shiners that they use for ice fishing got into that pond. You don't get small trout anymore and you don't get many big ones. You might go in there a couple of days and never get a fish. There's no more small trout. These shiners feed right offen the spawning beds. They eat the eggs. In turn the trout eat the shiners. So the adult trout are growing bigger. They used to run ten, twelve inches. The trout you catch in there now are weird looking things for a trout because they've got such a small head and a big body, weighing maybe two or three pounds. The type of the trout hasn't changed, because not enough little fish survive to breed.

Long Bog, Round Pond and those places used to run in there. They was all feeder streams, small feeder ponds. Now everything is cleaned. If they stopped all fishing on the feeder streams to the Kennebec, Dead River, Moose River and all of those places, leave them for spawning beds, you wouldn't have to have the fish hatcheries. But I have violated that rule more than the average.

One time when Father was manager of a club camp at Otter Pond, he had two parties that wanted to come for three weeks each to Ellis Pond Camps. He and Mother agreed that she and I could take care of them. I was around fourteen years old. Fred Marshall had the Tennessee Walker horse that was in our barn as much as he was in his own. Well, I loaded him up with packs and took him in to camp. I got there about twelve noon, unloaded the horse, gave him some grain, a little rest and sent him back home. We had a fire line telephone at camp so I called Mother and she went up the road about four miles with the oats to the point where the horse would come out of the woods. It is eight miles from Ellis Pond to The Forks and that old horse made the trip in one and a half hours. I had planned to come out and help Mother, but she said to stay and get some wood ready.

I didn't expect her for another day, but a little later I heard some voices and here comes Mother. She was leading the horse with my two younger brothers in pack baskets, one on each side of the horse and with more packs around the pack baskets. Also Mother had brought a young girl, Delora Pierce, to help take care of my brothers and do work around the camp.

I had two weeks work to get done before the first party come. I had three boats to paint and three canoes to get ready. Mow the grass, repair the old outside privy that the porcupines had chewed up. All the water had to be carried for washing and cooking. The spring was about two hundred yards from the camp.

The telephone line went dead so I had to take some wire and a few insulators and a hand made eight foot ladder and go look for the break. The telephone line was what they called a ground system. There was only one wire through white insulators hanging from trees. This line run three miles east to the Kennebec River near Elm Tree driving camp and connected on to this line that went to Indian Pond. I found the break near the river. It was a small job and when it was repaired I go down to the driver shack and called my mother. They were pitching a bateau and I watched awhile. I asked the foreman if he thought I could repair the rowboats at camp with the pitch and he said oh yes. He gave me about twenty pounds of the resin and this was the answer to leaks in our boats. I even touched up some of the canoes.

I made friends with a lot of animals at Ellis Pond. One day I was painting a boat and looked up to see a small doe looking at me. I kept on working not paying much attention and she nosed up to the bird feeder. I didn't have any bird seed so I had put out some old cake and bread for the birds. She ate some of the cake and went down to the pond for a drink. She walked within fifty feet of me. I started putting out sugar cubes and getting them a little closer to me. I started talking and she kept a close watch. I never made any moves toward her and she was coming closer all the time. (By the end of the summer) I would put her sugar out and whistle and she would come running. When we had people at the camp she wouldn't come out unless I was there and called her. The sports would get pictures of the deer taking sugar from my hand.

We needed no alarm clock at the camp. Two large red head woodpeckers used to come about every morning and light on the stovepipes and drum away. The noise could be heard clear at the other end of the lake. Shortly after dark the owls would start calling. One time I could hear one way off and I answered and waited for him to answer me. He come closer and we put the lights out and listened. We heard him land on the roof of the the camp and hoot a couple of times. I never got him to come back.

When the sports would come in from fishing, the guide and I would clean the fish down at the pond and leave the waste by the dock in the water. It was cleaned up every night. One night we were sitting on the porch and we heard animals fighting. We got flashlights and went down to the dock. An old mother coon and three young was having a fight with a wild cat. That old coon was in about a foot of water cleaning up the waste and the wild cat jumped on her. The coon won the battle. The coon near drowned the wild cat.

There was always porcupine around. They kept me busy replacing and repairing the outside privy. One night the sports heard a noise and they put on a flash-light and mother porcupine had brought three of her babies with her. This made the trip worthwhile for the women in the party. I was learning fast that fishing wasn't the only thing we had at Ellis pond. I had great plans for that place and this was when I started to get lumber for two new cottages when I found the camps had been burned. This was a great disappointment to me.

Our camps at Ellis Pond burned in 1929.

There was a logging camp down at the Otter Pond Landing on the Kennebec, and it was built all out of cedar, logs standing up. Beautiful logs. The loggers abandoned it so I took it into my head that I should take them logs into Ellis Pond, and build some more camps. So I had about a hundred of those seven-foot cedar logs on the team and I started to go into Ellis Pond. It was two days after Christmas. It was, from that logging camp, about thirteen miles. The game warden, he knew I was going in, he figured he'd ride in with me. So we went in. Foot of new snow so I had to take it easy with the horses and give them plenty of rest.

Well anyway, we got into the camp yard about two o'clock and I was talking with him, looking back, and he looked and he says, "Boy, Ellis Pond Camps are burnt." And I turned around and there they was smouldering, flat.

We were planning on staying there that night, unloading and everything, putting the horse in the hobble. Even the hobble that we had for the horses was burnt.

So the game warden said, "What are you going to do?" He said, "You can come and stay in my camp about a mile up the lake."

I said, "No, I'm going to feed the horses, let them rest a couple hours or so," and this was on a Monday.

Well, the fellow that burnt the camp he didn't want to leave his snowshoe tracks out in the tote road or anything. He went into the woods. Well, by just trying to get the horses out of the wind and the cold and put blankets on them and feed them and let them rest, I went into this black grove, and I could see these snowshoe tracks very plain. The new snow hadn't hit them. And on the toe of one of those snowshoes, it was the right one, was a splice on that bow, that they had put two pieces of wood and wound it with wire. And that print showed very plain. So I looked that over and started out to come home. I stopped the team a couple times and went up in the woods, and I could see them tracks. He stayed offen the road.

About four miles out there was a lumberman logging and he had a big set of camps there. I stopped the team, give them a little water, a little rest, and I went to get a cup of coffee and a sandwich or something in the cook camp. The men, the scalers and clerk hadn't come in. I went over to the office camp and was talking to the fellow that owned it and I looked up on the wall and there was a pair of snowshoes, one of them with that splice on it. I said to Mr. Hunnerwell, the jobber, I says, "Whose snowshoes are them, Frank?"

He told me the man's name.

I came out broken-hearted. I got home seven o'clock at night and I told Dad and Mother. And I says, "I know who done it."

Dad says, "Don't say a word to anybody. Now I don't want to tell anybody."

In about a day or so Father called me aside and told me. He says, "We know who done it. But he hasn't got a lot of money, he hasn't got anything. We've got three thousand dollars insurance."

Back in those days if you could prove that somebody did it the insurance company didn't have to pay. Now they're the ones who have to prove. So Father said we'd never be able to get the money. So it was never made known. I was a minor and it was what I had seen. The funny part of it was, the man who burned the camp had taken and old twelve-gauge single-shot shotgun out of the camp and evidently intended to take it, but when I had fed those horses and everything and I looked behind this tree, there was the shotgun. I have that gun in this house right now.

I loved that place in there. That's a big country to fish and hunt but it's ruined now. You're lucky if you pick up a trout out of that lake now. By putting the logging roads, automobile roads, truck roads close to all of them ponds.... Back in my time if forty people in the whole summer got in that area it was a big thing. Now you get them in a forenoon. Those little ponds and lakes can't stand the pressure.

There's too many people.

If the fisherman today can take five six-inch trout, he takes them. You don't see any real sportsmen now. You see more that's hogs than you really see as sportsmen. I don't say that I didn't do some of this stuff, but whenever I did I might be travelling in the woods or trapping, always carried a fish line along with me, a little bit of salt pork to catch a few fish to eat. I've gone to these little brooks and yanked out five or six to cook for dinner. I suppose that's just as bad as the guy today that goes in there with his family of kids and gets on to a brook and cleans it. But it's just too many people, and the pressure is just too great.

Charlie Bratton had a set of sporting camps there at Spencer Lake and I used to see as high as sixty people in them camps in the summer and probably twenty guides. One year I was running the post office and doing chores there. The mail used to leave every morning six days a week. It would leave Jackman, be taken across Attean Lake, up the Moose River to Attean Rips. At the first of the season I used to come out from Spencer eight miles to Spencer Rips, put the horses in the barn there, come down the river, pick up all the freight and everything and go back to the camps at Spencer. Then at night I'd

Spencer Lake Camps, Gerard, Maine.

take the mail that wasn't for us by boat down the lake six miles to the Twin Camps, they called it, and they'd come from King and Bartlett over Eustis way and get their mail. Later other men did the mail and I stayed right at camp guiding and whatnot.

There was two women in there at Spencer, and they wanted guides. Each one wanted to fish on the lake and everything and each one wanted a guide. So this Bill Hall was a guide there, and they asked me if I would work in. We guided these two women.

I'll never forget as long as I live. We was down at the

campground at the end of the lake, and this Bill Hall, I don't believe he was ever married, just a real trapper, a woodsman and a guide, well, he's cooking a fish chowder and I was getting other stuff ready. The women got talking politics.

One of these women spoke up and says, "What do you think of Calvin Coolidge, Mr. Hall?"

"Well," he says, "I'll tell you. He's smarter than a lot of people thinks. He didn't know nothing, but yet he knew it and he kept his damn mouth shut."

Well, we guided these women for a week. And so there was a send-off by everybody when they left, bid them good-bye like a family or something at the camp. Mr. Bratton was the owner of the sporting camp. He come out.

He says, "I want you people to know who you've been taking care of for the last two weeks. It's been an honor to me. Mrs. Calvin Coolidge."

Anyway, when she got ready to leave she put a fifty-dollar bill in my hand and said good-bye and she did the same to Bill.

Bill says, "I should be the one should keep my damn mouth shut."

Spencer Lake is about nine miles long. Beautiful fishing then. It was loaded with togue, but everybody was trying for trout. They claimed there was no salmon in that lake but as I'd be working around there I'd see a fish jump out front of the camps.

One day I come in and I said to Charles Bratton and

some of the other guides, "I see a salmon jumping out there in the lake."

"Oh for God's sake, Adams," he said. "There's no salmon and you know it."

I said, "Well, I know there is. I know a salmon when I see it jump. A salmon will go up into the air and come right back tail first. He don't come up and come down head first. A trout does."

They sat there and they didn't say anything. There was one game warden there. He didn't make any comment.

Went on the fall of the year and another guy and I had been getting the wood in for the camps. So we were cutting the wood and he got telling me about the "frost" fish that he knew ran between the first and the ninth of November between Spencer and Fish Ponds.

I said, "We ought to dip some."

Then I happened to think of this two-foot chicken wire, fine mesh that we had. I said we could make a net, which we did. We went out one night and that little stream between the ponds was just loaded with these frost fish. We dipped three barrel of them, we sent one to Hinkleys, an orphanage home, and we sent one out to the convent in Jackman, they had a lot of boarders, kids, and we kept a barrel for the place and different friends. But in this bunch there was about a four-pound land-locked salmon and they'd said there was no salmon in that lake.

We took it up and hung it on the nail there to show Charles Bratton, 'cause he'd always laughed at me. We didn't get up too early the next morning because we'd been up all night with the fish. In comes the game warden that morning before we were up and he looked at it. Here it is closed season for salmon.

He said, "Where'd you get that salmon, Azel?"

I said, "Right out of the lake here. He was caught in a net and killed himself."

"It's worth it to me to know there's salmon there," he says. "You told me last summer that you'd seen a salmon jumping."

But Spencer Lake isn't like it used to be. There used to be all kinds of fish and wildlife.

We had a boat at the camp, a cruiser, about twenty-four foot long. It had a big deck with a canvas top over it. It had a Lockwood-Ash motor in it. We used to be able to go out of Spencer and into Fish Pond.

At one time we could go up to Fish Pond just at sundown and we could count thirty-five, forty deer, maybe two or three wild cat. This was just on Fish Pond in August or July. And I have counted eighteen white deer, probably twelve that would be completely white, the rest red and white. I always claimed that they was crossing and breeding, but the biologists claim they never do. That many white deer, to be concentrated in one place I always thought they must be breeding, but they always said that white deer was something that very seldom happened and that they didn't breed.

There used to be a dam at the end of Spencer Lake and, while I was there, the Brassua Water Works was the name of the outfit that controlled it. We'd have a full head of water on Spencer Lake, beautiful for running the boat to Fish Pond and up and down the Lake, good fishing, and they would send a man in from The Forks. He'd walk in there about twenty miles to the dam and he'd unlock the gates and lift the gates. We'd be on the other end of the lake and we'd look. We knew about a day after we see the lake dropping that it was going to be hard getting around the lake and up into Fish Pond, so a couple of us fellows would volunteer to go down at night and shoot the lock off and drop the gates. This particular time a fellow by the name of Bert Morris, he and I took a canoe and we went down right in the daytime. It was pouring rain. We didn't want to be seen out on the dam. We walked through the bushes on the wing of the dam to get out there to shoot the lock off and drop the gate. On our way out, I was walking ahead, I see this silvery streak across in the bushes. I stopped.

I says, "What's that, Bert?"

"Oh," he says, "that's an eel going over land. You follow that streak of slime and if they haven't got into the lake you'll find an eel."

I followed it just a little ways and there was four eels, big ones, about three foot, three and a half feet long, and they were going, wiggling during the rain in their own slime. One would go ahead a ways and he'd stop, couldn't go anymore. He'd wait and another would crawl in the same place and over him and they'd go. We stood and watched them for five or ten minutes and I dare say they went over fifty feet through the bushes

Creative Survival

and on the land but they was headed for the water. They couldn't get up through the gate in the dam. I've told people about that and they laugh at it. They don't believe that an eel will go on land.

At one time eeling was really an industry on the Dead River.

There isn't many people in the town that remembers the eeling or the eel weirs that we used to have on the Dead River. This went on for seven or eight years. As a small boy of probably ten, twelve years old, I remember when the Ericsons, we called them the Germans, but they should have been Swedes, large men, six foot six or better, three brothers came from New York and started the eeling. Their eel weirs was made like snow fences, slat wood fences. They brought them in, roll after roll, by train. All three Ericsons would come up and work, and hire help getting those eel weirs set out across the Dead River. They was made in a way to catch the eels that was coming down from the rocks in the fall getting ready to go into the mud. They'd have a big box at the end of this weir, loaded down with rocks. They'd dig holes out of the river bed, sink the box, and they had rocks piled on the side to hold the box down, and as the eels would come down these weirs would funnel them into the boxes. Then on the other end of the box there was a scupper hole. The men would lower barrels down, pull up a door, fill the barrel with live eels, put burlap over the top and nail a hoop on.

Just about a half mile up the Dead River there was a cable that went across the river and they used to have a car that you could ride across. That car was there for the purpose of gauging the water and checking the flow of the water, and that's where they had the weirs. So they would catch these eels in the barrels and they had tongs that would go over the barrel and they'd use a little block and tackle, pull them up the hill. Then they had a one-plank-wide walk to push the barrels ashore. The eels would move at night, and the men would hang lights, kerosene lanterns, by every one of them boxes so that the eels would be attracted down in there. Around two or three o'clock in the morning the men would go out, fill the barrels and bring them ashore.

The peak of the eeling was the last of September when the water was getting cold. I've seen two big wagon loads leave around eight o'clock in the morning going to Lake Moxie to the railhead. In those days the Maine Central Railroad would go up around eight o'clock in the morning by Moxie, and continue up to Somerset and Rockwood. They'd turn and head back and at about one o'clock they would come back through Moxie. They'd always leave off a car at Moxie in the morning. I've seen twenty, twenty-five barrels of eels go in there a day. The last year that they operated the eel weirs I worked there filling barrels. I think they paid us thirty-five cents an hour. We thought that was big pay. Everybody else was paying twenty-five cents.

I still think that the eels run a lot to the Dead River, but nobody notices.

CHAPTER FOUR

Lumbering

It was something that has been practically forgotten on the Kennebec, the rafting of white birch logs.

I remember as a kid looking out my living room window at the lumbermen hauling white birch off the mountain. All winter long they'd haul. There's been a million and a half feet of white birch logs just this side the Marshall Hotel right in front of where our old home was there on the hill.

In those days, before they built Wyman Dam, they'd build these big landings out there. Then in early spring when they was driving logs down the Kennebec they would start making these rafts and haul the white birch into the river. Teams would drag the logs right into the water. They'd have long hardwood reaches, we used to call them, that they'd lay over the top of the logs and then they'd rope down around the white birch and tie them right up to the reaches. About every four or five big logs of white birch they used to have to catch a spruce or a pine coming down the river that belonged to the mills down below and put it in to float the others. Then they'd put two stanchions on each end with a big plank across on it and with pins in it and they had these big sweeps or oars and they'd be about twenty-five feet long. As they're going down the river if they'd want to steer the raft to keep from going ashore or anything, they'd use those sweeps to throw it over. And sometimes the small rafts, twenty-five hundred board feet, one man run it. He'd do the sweep. He'd have a set on each end, and he'd run back and forth.

They'd build rafts there with three to five thousand board feet. I recall Tim Moore and Norman Brag took a raft with fifty-two hundred in it down the Kennebec. It was a long raft, probably seventy-five, eighty feet long and fifty feet wide.

Well, as a kid, eight, nine years old, I used to be down there in the morning when them fellows would start and I thought I had to work and help them and everything. They used to give me a job with the pick pole, catching the pine or spruce going down for them. Then the old fellow running the gun there, in charge of everything, he most generally drove the team, keeping the thing going, I thought I had to be working with him all the time. I must have been in the way. He couldn't drop his mittens or gloves but what I'd be there to pick them up for him. I wanted to be of some use.

Well, it went on four or five years, and by the time I was fourteen or fifteen I was driving the team and hauling out. I kept at him, I wanted to ride down on the

Creative Survival

Birch Raft.

raft. He kind of felt duty-bound, I was always his shadow there, that he would let me go down. So they built a raft, and the water was good and high, and he said to the boys, "Do you want a helper this time?"

One of them says, "He hasn't any calk boots on. He can't go down."

I says, "I can get a pair!" and I take off over the hill and I find a pair of calk shoes about four sizes too big, wool socks, and I went down and I got on to the raft. I didn't tell Mother where I was going. Took about three hours to go the twenty-three miles with the raft.

When we got down to the old Starbird Mill in Bingham,

two fellows in a rowboat would see us coming. They had a rope coiled in the boat, one end tied to the shore, and as they rowed out they'd pay the rope off and they'd get out there and they'd have a loop and they'd throw it on one of the stanchions or posts on the raft. That rope was just the right length so that when the raft come down and the rope become taut she'd swing right into a slot there by the mill. Then we'd have to start untieing the raft, coiling the rope, hauling them reaches back. We used them same tie reaches for every raft.

We had an old Reo Speedwagon with a trailer behind, and we'd put that stuff on, and the ropes, go back to The Forks, work until dark making another raft. And there would be a couple of men up there already making rafts, so that there would always be a raft ready to be run down to the mill. Well, I thought that was a big thing in my life, that I rode that raft.

The next year there was two fellows running rafts. They had a good-sized raft made up and they was waiting for one of the men to show up. First thing they know they got notice that he was in the hospital. The old man says, "Well, it looks as though it's going to hurt us for a raft tomorrow, it looks as though I'll have to go."

His son, Tim Moore, says, "Why Azel can go down. He can help."

Well, that was the biggest thing that could ever happen! I was one of the sweepmen on the raft.

The last white birch that was put into the Kennebec River in rafts was put in right at the foot of Stand-Up Rips. The wood came out of the Cold Stream valley, and those were the last rafts that went down the Kennebec. They couldn't run big rafts from up there. There were probably only one to two thousand board feet in a raft.

As the dam come along (Wyman Dam at Bingham) they couldn't run any more rafts. They went from rafts to trucks. They used to put what they called a rocker on the back of a truck. From the rocker was a long pole attached to a sled behind the truck. That's all that would be on there. And then they would go right in to the woods and load the white birch on the rocker and sled. The only hill that they couldn't get up, they was taking it out of Cold Stream valley, was that one right by Marshall's Hotel. Well, I had a pair of horses. So I made a trade, a dollar a pull. They'd get stuck on that hill and I'd go over and hitch a pair of horses onto their truck and get them over. They'd get over that hill and they could get on to Bingham.

We were talking about the industry of the eels on the Dead River and the upper Kennebec. Really, the only other industry in the valleys was the lumbering. It became quite a task to get the logs offen those hills on either side of the rivers. If a person had movies today of what the old timers had to do to get wood offen those mountains it would be quite a movie. This is something that is a lost art.

I've seen everything from yarding with just a horse, dragging the logs out in the summertime, to bringing the logs out down the mountains on hay or sand and gravel with a team. Sand and gravel was dangerous. Quite a few horses and teamsters have been killed that way. The safest way was the snub ropes, snub warps we used to call them. You pick a big tree, solid, drill a big hole into it, and just below that hole off to the side just a little bit they'd have two more holes and they would put hardwood pegs in 'em. In the big hole up above they would have a lever, hardwood, about four or five inches in diameter and it would fit into that hole. Wind the rope

Creative Survival

around it and they'd come down with this lever on that rope running over the two hardwood stakes. They might have one complete turn, they might have two around the tree. They'd hitch that on to the back end of the sled and they'd go down the mountain with it. They'd use that where it would be too steep for using hay. They'd use the rope on sharp short pitches.

I've hauled in the mountains there when that we were coming down a mile and a half. We'd run on hay, and used the snub warp on steep slopes. We used to have men after every team went by would have to go and shake the hay up and lay it so it wouldn't pile up. The worst animal there was for working on a hay hill was the mule. When they'd start to run, instead of running like a horse one foot ahead of the other, they would go into a leap and strike with two feet. That would make the hay pile up in front of the nose of the sled and then they would take a wild ride down the mountain. They used to call it getting sluiced. When you'd sluice a team that was because you'd lost control.

You was asking about the time my team was sluiced.

Well, I was going to high school and there came a job of hauling pulp wood offen the mountain right across from the school. And of course I couldn't be driving the team then. So another teamster, he took my team and was hauling down this very steep hill and they run down with a couple of bridles under the runners, with a large load of logs. One of the chains broke loose on the bridle, and the horses just couldn't handle it. On the turn at the end of the road that whole load landed right on top of them two horses.

It was at recess and somebody came over and said they got a team sluiced over there on the mountain. Well, it was only about a quarter of a mile over to where it was, and I went over and they was digging the horses out. And the pole, the long pole between the two horses, it broke and it hit a tree and it split like that and it went right up underneath the harness between the harness and the skin of the nigh horse. Those horses you couldn't even see them, buried in pulpwood and I said, boy they're dead, they're gone.

We started to throw pulp to beat the band to get it off. We got it all off and got the chains off and everything and I started to unbuckle the harness. I got the nigh one's harness all off and I says, "You all right John? Are you going to get up?"

He grunted a little bit and stood right up. And the other one did the same. Not a scratch on them.

Now I'm telling you that taught me a lesson. I was some scared. I didn't realize how dangerous it was and the team belonged to somebody else; it really didn't belong to me. The team belonged to Otter Pond Camps and it would spend the winter in our barn. And this was a lesson that I learned.

Then they made a machine called the"snub machine". It was a device used with a brake system on a cable, a mechanical brake. They'd hitch one cable on to the back of a load of logs going down the mountain and they could set a brake and hold it at the right speed. The other end of the cable would be down at the foot of the mountain at what we called the go-back road and they would hitch this on to a team of horses and sleds coming back up. It would help haul the horses and sleds back up over the mountain as well as lower the load down. Where it says anchor posts on the drawing and shows holes on the plate of iron, they would drive posts or iron rods into the ground. On the end they could hitch a cable and anchor it to a tree.

All of these places had to have a go-back road. When you had a hay hill you had to have a different road to go back. And it was a long hard haul for the horses hauling these heavy wagons, sleds and drays up over these mountains to get up there to be loaded. As a rule two miles, two miles and a half back in the woods, that would be two trips a day. For pulpwood I've seen six or seven cords to a load come down to a pair of horses. Long logs, two thousand, twenty- five hundred board feet.

Where there wasn't too much lumber to come out, where it wasn't worth putting in a snub line and carrying in a lot of extra men for hay hills and things, they had what was called a bear trap bridle. I have worked on hills where that you'd put four of them on to come down a hill. This bear trap bridle had a long chain that would go around the front of the runner, we called it the raise. You had a patented link that would lock on to the main bridle. You would hold that and the horses would start ahead and run over it, it would catch on the front of the

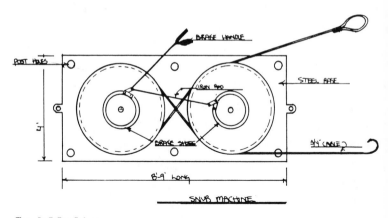

Snub Machine.
Susan Stanley drawing.

raise of the sled and drag underneath the runner. Most generally when you was doing that you had a helper. Sometimes you'd have to put two, sometimes three, sometimes only one. And it had to be pretty good teamstering, the judgement of the hill and everything. Couldn't be any guess work. The teamster had to know what he was doing. Otherwise he'd kill a pair of horses, kill himself very easy.

Today I don't know where you'd find a bear trap bridle. There might be one around the old home place somewhere but it would be throwed away. The bear trap bridle was the best bridle I think that was ever made to hold a pair of horses on a mountain.

Then they made one they called a marlin bridle. That was just a big chain. It had a slip link you could slide on the chain and then there was a narrowed-up place that you'd slide onto the link to hold it. They'd throw that on. That is something that you couldn't knock off easy if you got stuck. You'd have to dig it out. The bear trap you could kick that safety pin and drive off from it. The marlin bridle was really bad. I never used one and I wouldn't. And the reason I didn't was because my father told me. He says, "I don't want to see a marlin bridle in the barn."

Then they used another bridle. They called it the lazy man's bridle. Two chains in front of the bunk, then they'd throw a hardwood pole across and drag right under the runners. Well, a lot of things could happen there. If there were a rock in the road in the center or a high place or an old stump there that you dropped down on, it could break. When it would break, then you could take a ride. They were always hard to unhitch and get rid of.

I think that if you go through half of these towns, unless you talk to a man that's over fifty, if you ask him what a bear trap bridle is or if they know what a marlin bridle is they wouldn't be able to answer you.

These skidders that they come out with now, they can go anywhere, they can throw a chain around a thousand feet of lumber and come offen the mountain with it. They can do it and that thing don't get tired going back. It can go up the hill just the same speed as it come down. One man is doing the work that three or four were. And the chain saw come in about 1934, 35. Before that we used bucksaws.

There was a time, about 1930, when they'd bring long logs down to these big landings (on the Dead River). They'd have to have them all sawed up, and piled up. Then in the spring of the year they would throw (the wood) into the water when that the ice had gone out. We used bucksaws then.

This fellow that had the job, he wanted some cord cutters down on the yards, so three or four of us young fellows, I was about eighteen, we went down. If you're cutting wood on the yard especially after February you had to have two different blades. In the morning there would be frost in the wood and you'd have very little set. But when that the frost started coming out you'd got to have more set in your saw blade. So I always carried two, sometimes three bucksaws. We'd start cutting. Five cord a day, seventy-five cents a cord, and pile it. My biggest problem was piling; I didn't like to pile.

The jobber put out a prize for the one who could cut the most wood in a week. It wasn't what the prize was - it was a carton of Wings cigarettes that you could buy for fifty cents - it was just the principle of the thing. I averaged seven cord a day for six days. I got the prize, but I was burned out the next week, I couldn't get five. Now that seven cords a day took all the daylight and a little bit of dark. I'd be piling down there when the rest would be eating their supper in camp. For seventy-five cents a cord and a carton of cigarettes.

One thing always bothered me from that day on. A buddy of mine was a little taller than I was, but oh, wasn't he skinny. He kept on going. At the last of it, I'd quit, he was cutting seven cord a day every day himself. Doing it easy.

Back when I was first visiting the old-time logging camps my uncle was logging about eight miles back in the woods. He went in in the fall of the year and he was building a camp. My sister and I, we walked in to visit one weekend.

The men would bring in these logs full length, hemlock or spruce, two foot two foot and a half at the butt and they'd be forty foot long. They'd haul them in, bed the log down into the ground. Then they'd hew the top off and they'd bring another log. They made the sides right straight around and when they come ready to put the floor in they laid two poles up each side for joists. Then they cut small fir and spruce and they'd lay them top to butt, top to butt, floor it right across, fit it just as tight as they could. Then they'd take the adz and make the floor flat. I recall when we got ready to leave, they had got the logs up about so far and they decided to start cutting out the windows and the doors. Two men with a cross-cut saw would saw right down to get the doorway and the windows. They chinked the logs with moss.

The next weekend we went back in and the camp was complete. The men were moving in and they was building a hovel for the horses and they was building a cook camp.

The thing that is recorded in my mind from the old days was the bedding they used. They'd put a row of bunks, one would be about a foot, foot and a half off the floor the full length of the building. Then they'd put another one just about three feet up above that, the full length. There'd be room for about twenty-five men on the bottom bunk and twenty-five men on the top. They'd just put hay all down on that. Then they'd roll out one big old wool spread that would go the whole length and that was the mattress and the men could sleep on that. Then they had another spread they rolled the full length up on top to cover you up. So when you go to bed at night you either crawled up through underneath or went up and crawled down. You never had any pillows. You'd take your jacket or something and roll it up to put under your head. They used to have an idea then that to keep from getting lice and everything they'd use camphor. Some of those men, they'd be family men and go home on weekends and didn't want to get lousy they would bring camphor in and shake it around on the beds on the area where they sleep, and oh did that camp used to stink. I never did sleep under a gang blanket like that. I'm glad I never did.

When I got going into the camps it was a little better. They used to put a board up between the bunks. You could use anything you wanted for bedding, hay or go out and get fir boughs and lay them. My dad could lay fir boughs and make a bunk that would sleep just as good as a bed. Just by laying the boughs just so, the heavier ones first and the smaller ones on the top. It would be very springy. Then put your blankets over that. That was in the late twenties.

I got pretty clever with an ax. It was one of the things I wanted to learn. These old timers in the woods, they chopped a lot with axes then, no chain saws or anything, and my being a young man in the camp the old fellows would come out and want me to help them sharpen their axes. They'd say to me, "Give me a little turn, give me a little turn."

We'd go out into the dingle. There'd be a big grindstone there, long handle on it you'd put both hands on to turn. Them old timers used to use double-bitted axes. They'd stand right up on the frame of the grindstone and get their hands out on the ax and bend their knees and boy they'd bear down. One old fellow by the name of Bill Nugent taught me a lot about axes.

He said, "The first thing you've got to have a sharp ax. You just don't grab an ax and think you're going to do something with it. It's got to be sharp. Then you got to get used to it. It's got to be part of you."

Well, it was true.

Anyway, I'd have to turn the grindstone for those fellows sharpening the axes. And I'd watch them, how they whet them up, and I've seen old Bill roll his shirt sleeve up and shave the hair offen his arm.

"There," he'd say. "If I couldn't skin a mouse without waking him up I wouldn't use it."

The pride of the woodsman then was sharp tools. Nothing like that anymore.

These are the ways that the camps was handled back in those days, in the twenties. The logs was all cut with crosscut saw and axes and roads was built for teams and horses. Then they started using bulldozers, tractors. Building roads back into the woods. They started using trucks, trucking the wood out.

They opened the country up and they talk about the predators of the animals, the wild life. The predators of them is the man. It wasn't that he was out killing them outright but he was just opening the country for the tremendous pressure on these animals. Hunting, fishing, our fishing is gone. Back when I was a young fellow very seldom would you see anybody go fish them streams around The Forks. If they wanted a little mess of trout ... there wasn't too many people who would go to get a little mess of trout out of a brook or stream or beaver bog. Those beaver bogs and those streams in my day they were feeder brooks. They were the fish hatchery for those areas. But today they're cleaned out. I am in hopes that somebody will close all of those feeder streams and brooks to fishing and then control the lake fishing. Because the pressure is so great now on the sport fishing in those areas it's terrible.

In the late lumber camps, the last one I was in, they had running hot and cold water, showers, flush toilets, the men drive their automobiles to the camp, then they drive out to within a quarter of a mile of their work, where they're cutting. And this new method is probably better for the men, but I don't see where it helps the hunting, fishing or wood lot. Another ten years the pine board as lumber is going to be gone. It is going to be one of the most expensive lumbers that we have. But nobody wants to stop. They're really cleaning it.

My father and my uncle Charles Wilson was logging in beyond Tomhegan Stream. When I quit high school in my third year, I come home and said I'd quit school. Dad said, "Well, that's your decision. But don't think you're going to hang around here. If you aren't going to school, go to work somewhere. Get yourself a job."

So I didn't say a word. On Monday morning I went into camp. I wouldn't ask my father for a job, but I asked my uncle.

He said, "Yes, you can go swamping roads."

So we were building trails and swamping roads and there was choppers in there, and my uncle was giving me three dollars a day, and board. That was good money.

My uncle had a hundred and fifty men in there. He had a cook who used to drink quite a bit. He used to buy this pure vanilla extract by the case. One afternoon about two o'clock my father come up into the woods where we were about a mile and a half from camp and he says, "Azel, you take a couple of men and go down there and get supper ready."

I says, "What's the matter with Doc?"

"Oh," he says, "he's drunk."

He'd been drinking for a week and his cookees had been covering for him, doing the work, but they couldn't cook, bake or anything.

I landed down there. There was no potatoes peeled, no bread made, no cakes made, no meat cooked, no beans baked ahead. Well, we started in on that dingle. That dingle, that's a shed next to the cook shack. Got a side of beef, about half frozen, started cutting it up all into steaks. We had two big ironclad cook stoves there and I directed the boys, "Start frying them steaks."

We smothered them in onions and we put a wash boiler down on the hearth and as the boys cooked the steaks they'd throw them in that wash boiler. I went to making biscuits and then gingerbread so they'd have something for dessert. The boys mashed the potatoes, throwed in a lot of canned milk and salt and pepper and butter and we had a boiler full of that. We always had peas and corn for vegetables.

Well, most generally about six o'clock you kicked that door open and hollered "Come and get it." We was about a half hour late, but we had the supper ready for them.

Those fellows begin to rave. This was on a Wednesday and I had made up my mind that I was coming out Saturday so some of the boys stayed and done the cooking for the men that stayed in the camp. When I got home my father started giving me the devil about being too extravagant, giving them steak and everything.

"Well," I says, "go get somebody else to do the cooking." I said, "A man is only going to eat so much. If he enjoys it it's better than having boiled meat, boiled meat all the time."

Mother said, "He's right."

My mother taught every one of us boys how to cook. I think she spent more time with us boys learning us to cook than she did with my sisters.

My uncle left me there in that slot for two weeks,

cooking. But I did learn how much flour a hundred and fifty men will eat in a day. A barrel of flour weighs a hundred and ninety-six pounds and we used to knock in a head of a barrel of flour every morning between ten and twelve. Six days a week. Sunday, no. People wouldn't believe. You're packing lunches, make all your bread, make your doughnuts, your pies, your cakes, and I used to make pancakes in the morning. We used to buy a syrup that was just as good as the maple syrup that you get now. They called it commercial cooking syrup, something like that. We used to buy it in five-gallon cans. And keep a jar of molasses on the table. I'd get up in the morning and it always seemed easy to mix a batch of pancakes. And I had the boys so that they could fry them.

To get up and get breakfast for men to eat at quarter of six you had to get up at three thirty. If you had beans you had them baking all night. You'd have fried potatoes. You didn't have many fried eggs or anything, but we used to have ham a lot. You couldn't keep eggs. But oatmeal. I'd make three different kettles of oatmeal. One I'd have cooked and flavored with a little vanilla in it and mix some other grain into it, and one I'd have about four big tablespoons of molasses in it, and then I'd make one with the syrup in it. They'd have their pick.

The Canadian boys was very heavy on sweets, pies. You'd have pies on the tables and whatnot and some of those boys would come in and they'd start and eat the pie before they'd eat the meat and potatoes and beans. And then at night after supper we would load one table with pies, cakes, cookies and things and anybody who wanted could come in and have a lunch. We'd have a big teapot on the stove. Some of those guys go in there at eight, nine o'clock and have a lunch before they'd go to bed.

So that took a lot of flour.

One summer I went up to the Dead River Dam, eighteen mile up the river from The Forks. Fellow was rebuilding the old wood dam all over. I hired out as axman, broad ax. Boy, there was some good hewing men there.

I didn't like to cook too well unless there was nothing else to do. So if I hadn't been good with an ax in those days I would have been in the cook camp. You take a bunch of old men like that, they're awful cranky, awful hard to satisfy with their food. Their tastes are changing and they're not burning the energy that they used to, and a lot of them got sickness building into them and they don't realize it.

I had worked with my father building camps and everything and he'd be watching me do something.

"What are you doing it that way for?"

He'd show me once. That was it. I had to go on from there. He wouldn't take something I was doing and finish it or anything. He would just show me.

So anyway I hired out. This Danny Burns, he was a hardheaded old dam builder and bridge builder and what not. We all went up to work. They were hauling in big pine logs, sixty foot long and they had to hew two sides to lay them water tight.

Creative Survival

He says, "You fellows lay out your hewing beds in this area here."

I seen the fellow bring down some skids. I said, "Bring my log out."

The first log I done, some of these old hewmen, some of them fifty, sixty years old who had spent their life at it, come over to watch the kid. I'd skin the bark offen it, then I'd roll the log so that it would be the least hewing and straightest and I'd snap the line. My dad had taught me how to hew. Scarf a log, we called it then. Cut in to the line right square on the log and then after you'd gone the full length you'd take your big broad ax, twelve inches wide at the blade, and you'd swing it and split that line, right plumb. Well, when I come down the old man says a good broadaxman makes no chips flying at all. He just splits the line and when he gets down to the end that whole outside piece of wood and bark flops off. But cutting in, you see, gives it relief. After that first log they was putting me in the top jobs, hewing, making gates and things like that. Well, I thought that that was just natural.

Come Thanksgiving and I come out, Father says to me, "You better take snowshoes back if you're not coming back before Christmas."

I did. They laughed at me when I come into camp. "Where you going? North Pole?"

"No," I said. "Don't weigh much. Could get a snowstorm anytime now." They laughed at me.

Two days before Christmas we was finishing up. I said to one of the other fellows, "Let's get out of here

Snapping the line

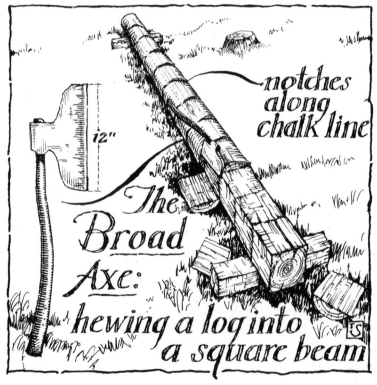

12"

notches
along
chalk line

*The
Broad
Axe:*

*hewing a log into
a square beam*

tonight. Are you too tired?" I says, "We can walk down. This lull, no air moving, it looks like we're going to get a storm."

We had no radios or anything then, no contact with weather stations or anything. When we asked Danny Burns, he says, "I want you boys to stay around. We got to put some sleds away tomorrow and we got to do this and that."

I says, "You don't need sixteen of us."

Well he got kind of mad, thinking that I wanted to slough off on my work and one thing and another. I stayed. Four o'clock the next morning I tried to open the door. I couldn't open it, the snow was against it.

I woke the rest of the crew up and weren't they disgusted, because here we are headed home for Christmas. Eighteen miles and only one pair of snowshoes. Sixteen men.

I'd give anything to have pictures today to see what they improvised for snowshoes. They didn't have rawhide or anything for stringing, but they had a lot of burlap bags. So they used hemlock boughs, trimmed them off, shaved them down, grooved them to put a crosspiece in , steamed and bent them, and then they'd put the burlap to them. They found a bunch of old leather tops and they had enough to make lashings. Some of the snowshoes didn't last more than four or five miles. We had twenty-two inches of snow. There was an old driving camp on the river. Another fellow and I got down to there and I called on the fire line to The Forks. They got word to my father that these men were all coming and to bring a canoe up so that we could get across the river.

They come up with a couple of canoes, three or four teams with sleds. I told Father that if they had some snowshoes they could go up and meet the men, because they are wallering in twenty-two inches of snow. About eleven o'clock that night we was all at The Forks, but we had left early. I was played right out because I was breaking the road all the way with my snowshoes. I did swap with my buddy Benny Durgin for a while but he only weighed a hundred twenty pounds and he wasn't going to bottom, and I weighed about a hundred and sixty. But we made it.

In the spring of the year when that they would be running the pulp wood out of Cold Stream and offen the mountains they had these various dams. They had this dam called Number Five dam up on Johnson Mountain, and the pond would flow back about one hundred acres. Used to be a lumber camp there. They was logging down below and they was using the storage water for floating the pulp out of these small streams, Tomhegan and Cold Stream.

To lift the gate of the dam they used to have a pry system with long, long twenty-foot spruce pries that you'd put in and bend down. You'd push one down and then the other guy would put his pry in and he'd come down. And you'd be going like that to lift the gate. The gate was twenty, twenty-four feet high. I could lift that gate alone by coming down on the pry and then standing on the pry and putting the next one in and then transferring my weight over on to that one.

So, about quarter of six this morning the telephone rang and they wanted us to lift the gates. This fellow by the name of Ed Burns, he and I were tending the gate. I says, "I'll go out and do it. You get breakfast."

So I pulled on a pair of old rubbers, I went out. It had rained. This was in April, it was during my Easter vacation. I was still in high school. I went out and I lifted the gates all right and I started to walk in. An old log that the dam was built out of, they had left the bark on it. As I stepped on it that bark skun off and I dropped down twenty-four feet right into the sluice gate. There was a boom log come up on each side to guide the pulp or the water out. There was about a half-acre pool below the dam. I don't know how long I was there from the time I tunked in, but I was across the pool on the other side washed up on the bank when I come to.

I was on the wrong side of the stream so I had to go up around and come across the dam again. I could see where that piece of bark skun right off. My chest was one big blood blister right where it hit. Broke my ribs. So I got up to the camp and told Ed what happened. Oh, he got scared. He called for help and they sent a car after me. But he and I decided that we would never tell that I was alone. It could have happened even if we had been together. But Ed felt bad about that. Well, I got pneumonia from it and I had six ribs and my collarbone broke.

I just got healed up from that, working around the farm there to home. We had an old mare horse and she was a kicker. I was cleaning the stall out and I'd let her out. She came back in and she got into the wrong stall. I went along and tapped her with the shovel, said, "Get out of there."

Them feet flew and she struck me right here in the chest. She had shoes on. I went right out of the barn. I come to, I was out in the manure pile. Four more ribs broke.

So the old body took a lot of abuse.

In those days they peeled the fir, the spruce, and the popple to make it lighter. The spruce used to peel and run a couple of months from the time it was cut. I say it would run. That meant that you could peel it. The bark adheres after the sap starts going into the leaves. When the sap is going into the tree you can peel it. When it starts going into the foliage then the bark starts sticking on the tree. You could peel popple, if you got a month you was lucky.

The bark was waste and it was cheaper and easier to peel the logs in the woods than it was to float them down the river and try to peel them later. When that they made machines that would peel the logs down at the mill it really hurt the environment. It hurt the woods because there was nothing left to make new soil and it hurt the streams, all that bark falling off in the river. Lumber was one of the worst things, with the tannic acid from the bark, that could happen to the river and it did affect the spawning of the fish.

There was this Ralph Pierce in the town. He was always a clerk and a scaler for the S.D. Warren Co. in the woods. He asked me one time, I got out of school a couple weeks early, I was probably sixteen or seventeen years old, to go in with him. They called us counters. Each week we would have to count how many logs each crew had cut and peeled. The company used to pay the cutters around ten, twelve cents a tree for cutting and peeling. And if the men stayed and sawed the tree up they probably were paid seventy cents a cord and five cents more for peeling.

The S.D. Warren Company was cutting popple offen Hollingsworth and Whitney land. They had a camp in there near Rock Pond. Where they were cutting was on Gold Brook. So there was three crews up in there that I'd count the trees that they'd cut. I'd have to get the count in Friday so they could be paid off Friday night.

There was one pair of men that was staying in a tarpaper shack and they'd got dishes and blankets and everything so they didn't have to walk in. They were staying right up there in the woods. The Blueberry boys, Adelair and Joseph Blueberry. I went up and I think I counted twenty, twenty-five trees first time. The next time I come back, no more trees cut. So I walked five or six miles back to camp and I told Ralph.

Well, Ralph sent me back and he said, "Go up and find out what they're doing, if they're there."

He told me where the camp was, because I hadn't got clear up to it. The camp was right on the shore of Gold Brook. I went up to the camp and there was a little fire

Scalers.

outdoors and it was still smoking. Inside the camp there was a whole bunch of little bottles setting on the window sill. I come out and I looked and I could just see some movement of somebody way up the stream. I went up and there they were, panning gold.

They had a dish pan and a shovel and a fry pan. At that time the average wage for a man was around two dollars a day. Gold was selling then for around five, six dollars an ounce. They was making more money panning gold than they would cutting wood, so they panned gold.

They used to have log drives on the Kennebec. There was a buddy of mine, about a year older than I was, Chester McKay, his father was the walking boss on this drive coming out. So we go up to work on the drive spring vacation and during the summer months. Pretty big drive - it lasted quite a while. Well the camp we stayed in was a lean-to affair, one large open building, log building with bunks in it. They used to haul logs right in next to that lean-to, twelve, fourteen, fifteen foot long. And they'd build fires, and the heat would reflect in.

The cook didn't have a stove, just open fire. We didn't stay long enough and he never had a stove in that cook camp. But he had this open fire and he'd have a bean hole to make the beans in. We had this one cook, he could roast meat and potatoes in a bean pot in the ground and boy, they was some good. A lot better than boiling them over a fire. And he made biscuits, cakes, pies and cookies with a metal baker, a tin baker, by the side of the fire.

They had three of these log drivers' camps down from Indian Pond along the Kennebec, and they had the twenty-four foot bateaux- they had some bigger than that- most the them that we used were twenty-four footers. They used to have four men on the oars and a man on the bow and a man on the stern, and they'd go back and forth ferrying men across to work a jam over here or anywhere they wanted to go in the river. Those bateaux, when they got the pitch of the water out of Indian Pond Dam just right, they would run the river where the white water rafting is now. (The amount of water flowing in the river was regulated by the dam at Indian Pond.) Those days even if the bateau started leaking you'd work what high water there was, probably six hours, and when the water level went down then was when you'd pull the bateau out and pitch it.

They used to get a fire going and have these irons, old wagon tire irons, they'd stick them in the fire and get them hot. They'd have about four irons by the fire all the time. Bateau bottom side up, they'd burn the pitch that they had right into the wood, smooth it off. They used to call it ironing the bateau. Then they'd have some pitch mixed up with some lard, about ten pounds of pitch, you'd put about two pounds of lard in it. These oldtimers pitching a boat remind you of a cook. They would be boiling the pitch and they'd keep putting the lard in. They'd put a little stick in and they'd have a pail there with some cold water in it and when that they dropped the pitch into the cold water and it would stay just tacky enough to not break - the pitch that you'd buy was hard and it would break easy - well, they'd get it just pliable enough so as not to break. Then they'd take rags tied on to a stick, dip it into the kettle, and they'd pitch that whole boat all over, the whole bottom of it. That would be good for another week, ten days, driving over the rocks. And when it would start another leak, "Well, we've got to pitch the boat again."

Those boats could really stand the drive, the pounding in the rocks and everything. This is something that is lost now.

Everybody thought that they was better than the others. Kennebecers, they thought that they were the tops in the log drives and in the woods and then the Penobscot...the East Branch wasn't as hard as the Dead River. And then you have the Machias River people. The log drivers on the Machias prided themselves that they was the best. And they started the log-rolling competitions and what not. Machias always wanted to be recognized as the top. They had a pretty rough little river there that they worked. Downeasters, they were pretty proud men too.

That summer on the Kennebec was my first to go out on a log drive. They had one fellow there, for a big man he was the lightest man on his feet I ever see. First week or two that I was there he had me in water more than I was up on the logs. He'd take a cant of a log, give it a snap, throw you in.

They'd give you a promise that if you'd come up and help get the wood out of a stream, out of the Enchanted or Stony Brook or some of those, you'd have it easy going down the river. Bringing the rear down the river is what they called it. That's so that every one of these companies, two or three different companies, would get all of their wood. Sometimes they would have to hang a drive. When you 'd hang a drive you got to wait to next year. The water left you. If you had to hang a drive, you come into the fall and the ice makes and then when the freshets come in the spring of the year they wipe the rivers clean of the ice cakes that the logs and the pulp wood is froze in. That's when you get into trouble downriver. That ice with logs in it is like reinforced concrete. And a lot of that wood goes right into the ocean.

In the summertime, the early summer, was when you'd bring down the rear. The first one I went on was up on Spencer, and down the Dead River. I never forgot it. I was about sixteen years old. In what we called Spencer Gut was a narrow stretch with high ledges. They'd dumped too much lumber into the stream above and it plugged. There was forty-foot pine and spruce standing on end and all crossed up in there and everything, and down below there was very little water running. It was building up, backing up water. The plug was there about four or five days. They sent a man out and he come in with about fifty pounds of dynamite and fuses and caps. There was an old fellow who was driving boss whose name was Brint Smith. I don't know if that was his first name but that's what we called him. And some of the old timers looked it all over and they said, "The only way we're going to get that, we're going to plant a charge of dynamite down in the bottom right out there in the middle."

"Well, young fella," Brint says, "will you go down? We can pull you up right out of there easy. We'll put a rope on you. You put that dynamite in there and then you light that fuse. And you come back and we'll pull you up over."

Well, I got down there and all ready to walk out onto the logs and I could hear "Crack!" up above in the jam.

I was pretty nervous but I went out. When that I got out there I pushed the dynamite in and it fell into the water, but the fuse just stuck up and I lit a match and I took off. They'd soaped the fuse anyway so that it would burn. I was making more slack than they was taking away, but they pulled me up over. When that went off - I can see it now -those big spruce and pine were going like match sticks through that gut when they started going. Of course we didn't know about it till later, but when that jam of logs and water hit The Forks they went right over the road there. There was that much come down through.

I would work in the spring for a couple of weeks on the drive bringing down the rear. But you learn kind of fast. If you've been on a good dry rear, not much water and you're just lugging wood to get it into what water you had, you learn not to go on the drive that year.

In those days they used to have fin booms on the river. There used to be a fin boom just below the bridge on the West Forks side and it was six, seven hundred feet long. It was anchored on the west side of the Kennebec. It came down almost to Marshall's camp. When there wasn't too much current coming down the river there was just enough to work against the fins to put that boom right against the shore on the opposite side down at Marshall's. As a kid I jumped on to that and walked up the boom and got off up where the old covered bridge used to be. There was one at that location, there was one about a mile below that. I know of about five or six that was between The Forks and Bingham. And they had them below Bingham.

The way this boom was, it was two logs wide. They would drill holes in the two ends of the logs and put a rope in there and drive in a wooden peg to hold it. Then they'd tie the ends of the logs together. In the high water they didn't want the logs to go into the sandbar back of Marshall's and pile up, so they put another log in such a way that when the current come down and hit the log it pushed the boom out. This was what they called a fin boom. They used fin booms and solid booms to sort the logs, some would pull the logs to one side of the river to be drawn out to a mill and some was to let the logs through to go down further. About 1920 it was nothing to see the river run plumb full of logs, millions and millions of board feet of logs, and beautiful pine.

All of these logs was marked. And in those days they used to chop the logs with an ax to mark. There might be an X and three slashes, or it might be a V and two slashes and these all meant different lumber companies. These logs was all coming down the river together. And they would hit a place, come to a mill and this fellow would have a boom there and would be getting his logs. He had to let the rest go by. Every now and then there would be a little rumble among the mill owners and the lumbermen. They had had some of their lumber stolen. Then they stopped chopping to mark and started painting. They would paint on the end of the logs. This was one way that everyone could use the river. But there was always problems.

It was 1920, 21, they were logging up the Dead River,

Enchanted Stream. It was an outfit by the name of Boyd and Harvey. Long logs; it was a tremendous operation for those days. Probably five hundred men in the woods, cutting and swamping roads. They'd take the trees full length, but they would top them off at eight inches. Anything under eight inches was throwed away in the woods. They was hauling those logs out with log haulers, the old steam log haulers.

They'd yard the logs out and put them on landings in the woods in those days. As they cut the wood they'd yard it out and they'd swamp a big road up through, what they'd call a log hauler road. They'd make these big landings, one right side of the other. They'd set the sleds with horses. They'd have cant dog crews loading the logs. In those days the log hauler would take eight, ten sleds with about two thousand feet of logs on each sled. They would haul the logs about eight miles down to the flat, right to the edge of the Dead River, which they called the First, Second and Third Field from where Salmon Stream comes in down towards Durgin Corner. Those fields would be right plumb full of logs that they'd unload from the log hauler.

In the spring of the year and when they had ice on the shores they'd start rolling the logs and loading the river. And then the high water come and take them down the river. Well Sir, I've seen that river so full of logs you could hear it crunching and roaring and pushing into the banks and rocks.

There was one boy in our class whose name was Tom Harris - he got drowned later in life on the Kennebec. He grabbed a pole and went clear across the river running and jumping from one log to the other. He stayed over there quite a little while and the logs began to thin out. He started coming back. He made it, but he had to do some fast work.

Then the pulp wood come in. They'd haul right on to the river and unload all winter long onto the ice. There at The Forks I've seen as many as twenty trucks unloading at once, each throwing six, ten cord of pulp wood right into the river. It was going down, freezing, backing up. That wood in that ice, especially down back of Marshall's and through to Caratunk, was all jammed in the ice, just like reinforced steel in concrete. So when the heavy water came in the spring of the year, run off, anchor ice, she'd pile up. From Caratunk to about three miles up I've seen ice piled up to the tops of the telephone poles, to the wires. They're controlling the water now so that it keeps the river open and thawed out.

They're controlling it now in Moosehead and Indian Pond. Putting that power station in so that the water doesn't have the frost in it. It's warmer. When they open the dam there and start the water wheels generating they're letting enough water come down through so that it keeps the river clean. So these power plants and these dams have helped a lot.

When that cement dam was put in on the Dead River, about 1945, that helped a lot. Before that dam was put in that river would be froze up full of ice, full length and then a quick runoff in the spring of the year would start plowing that stuff down. This gravel bed that is right across from Marshall's where the two rivers come to-gether - I've seen boulders that couldn't fit in this room come down out of Dead River, rolling down with the ice, and it would leave them there. All over the river bed there you would see these big boulders.

Well, that was just a natural place for logs when they come down to jam. So we would have to go out and hand-drill holes into these boulders probably a couple of feet deep and put dynamite in. We'd wade out and get out there, two men striking with hammers and one man holding the drill and turning it. You got the hole in the boulder two feet, two feet and a half, load it with dynamite and hope it would blow it. It didn't work with primer cord fuse like it does with electric cords today. Now you wire off two holes with an electric cap and they go together. Then it was almost impossible to have two fuses go together. So as a rule we'd only use one hole. We'd soak the fuse and light it and wade ashore and wait for it to go off. Sometimes it didn't go off, and that was the dangerous part, you'd go back and see why it didn't. Sometimes we'd leave them overnight before we'd go back.

They'd blow them rocks so that they wouldn't be jamming up the logs coming down. Since they've had that cement dam in I've not seen the rocks in those rivers.

I was maybe seventeen, eighteen years old. I worked in a lumber camp in on Ten Thousand Acres in by Horse-shoe Pond. There was a fellow there named Harry

Salters that was in there for the Hollingsworth and Whitney Co., and he was cutting fifteen thousand cords of pulp in there. Well, usually they cut about three thousand cord a year or four, but they had made this a big cut and they was pushing to do it in two years. So in order to cut it and get it out of there they went to the log haulers.

This log hauler that we used then was made by the same company that made the steam log hauler but they had adapted the gasoline engine to it. It was called the Lombard Log Hauler. The other one was called the Lombard Log Hauler, but it was steam. They wanted some teams to go in on the sprinkler wagon. There was a fellow by the name of Robinson that was taking charge of the hauling. He had a son just a little older than I was. He knew I had a good team and he wanted me to go in on the water truck with him. Sprinkler trucks.

This was in the wintertime. Every night they'd go through with four horses all over the road, and they dragged what they called a rutter. This rutter was pulled by a team and had two knives about twelve inches wide, like little plows, to cut grooves in the ice road. The rutter would shave the ice right off so the grooves would be about four inches deep, and these grooves would hold the log hauler wheels in place, like a railroad track holds a train. We would come along behind with the sprinkler truck and we would sprinkle the whole width of the road. We were hauling tanks of water with a four-horse team. We used to load the water wagons with a horse pulling the water up in barrels up a sluice and when it come up so high the end of the barrel tipped over. It was on a hook. One man would stand up on the top of the ramp and throw the barrel back in the sluice. Another man down at the bottom of the sluice had a pole. He'd fill the barrel, take the horse and haul the barrel back up the sluice. We'd take about forty barrels of water to the time. Then on the back of this big wooden water tank that was on sleds there was about a four-inch hole, you drive a wooden plug in it. So when you get to a place that you wanted to sprinkle, you'd knock the plug out. Then after you knocked the plug out you had little sliding doors that if you wanted to shut it off or something the fellow driving the teams he'd holler, "Shut off the water."

He'd slide them little boards down in front of the hole and when you wanted water you'd pull them up. So you really only used the plug while you was filling up and until the first application.

We used to work all night sprinkling roads and icing them up. In the morning the log haulers would head out and they would do their thing. We'd sleep all day, but you couldn't sleep in a lumber camp. A lot of men sick, colds, coming in and out. But I enjoyed it. I was young and accepted by the older fellows, and I was working with a fellow about my age and they thought we was doing a hell of a job and I guess we did. They got the pulp out of there.

On these Lombard Haulers there were runners out in front and a man set out there in a little cupola steering. Now this was the first gasoline log haulers. Later on they was doing their steering from the cab. The fellow that was operating was doing the whole thing. But in the early models he had conductors and tenders in the back to tend the sleds and everything. A lot of those jobs they used to work night and day.

A tender and a conductor was in back of the log hauler and would hitch up the sleds and everything. A man running the log hauler couldn't be looking back as well as looking ahead. They didn't have the big rear-view mirrors they have now. So the conductor was to watch, and if he was running nights, he would have his signals with lanterns. So this fellow riding in back, the tender, something go wrong he'd wave the lantern. Well, if the conductor missed it, there might be a lot of trouble. They'd get it stopped and go back and get the load squared away.

The last log hauler that I can recall we used up to Moosehorn up to Washington County above Jacksonville, Maine. I wasn't even supposed to go up there.

The fellow that owned the log haulers then and was doing the lumbering, Earl Taylor, he lived about twenty-three miles from us. Well, when they got the log haulers up about half way up the Airline, that's Route 9 now, they stopped for the night. The next morning the guy that was going to operate the log hauler, he goes out to crank the gasoline engine. Instead of using a rope like he was supposed to, with a couple of men to roll the engine over, he gets down in there between the bumper and the front of the engine and uses his foot to kick it down. And she kicked and throwed him out and broke his leg. So they had to haul him to the Bangor hospital. A cousin of mine, Milton Morris, he had run the hauler a little bit and they asked him to go up. He told Earl Taylor he'd like to have me as a conductor. So I went. We had two crews, hauling night and day.

My cousin and I stayed in Jacksonville, Maine, and the guy that we picked as tender was this Penny Giel that we was boarding from. This kept us out of a lousy lumber camp. I'm telling you it was an experience.

This was offen the Airline, hauling through Moosehorn down to the Machias River. In those days they'd come out with the crawler tractors. That was the last that that I know of a log hauler being used.

The fellow that we was boarding with, his wife, she might have been thirty-five years old, she was cutting pulp. When we went up there they were cutting pulp together. She'd get up and get us breakfast, or supper, and she'd take off into the woods with her buck saw and her ax for the day. Our lunch was put up. She used to average a cord a day at the stump and she was being paid three dollars a cord.

Penny Giel and his wife lived in a log cabin. Everytime I go up through there I stop in. The last time I went up her husband that was with us, he was dead. But Penny's wife is still living, she's pretty old. You go in there any time and "Oh, you stay! We're going to have a pan of biscuits."

Wonderful old lady.

CHAPTER FIVE

The Depression (1931-1942)

I went over to White River Junction before I was married intending to go to school. I was going to attend the Clark Preparatory School after I finished high school in The Forks. That must have been about 1930. I wanted a job and I didn't want to work for my uncle or any of my relatives so I hired out with an old one-armed paperhanger. He had a room at the Adams House.

There was a big dormitory at Dartmouth College, and this old paperhanger took the contract to paper every room in that dormitory. He hired me to work with him. They furnished the paper. Nothing was in the rooms, the painting was done. There was usually two doors, one window, sometimes two, and a steam register in each room. They'd disconnect the registers. When we come in the paper was there and that was it.

We used to do four rooms a day. Two of us, and one only had one arm. He could cut paper, match, tell me how to roll it out. I was darn busy! But we didn't work an eight-hour day then. We'd work ten, eleven hours. If we done four rooms, I got four dollars.

He got four dollars a room himself and he paid me a dollar of that. 'Course he furnished the paste and the tools and he was teaching me the trade. And it was a trade I used long after I was married and living in the town of Jackman. Come the spring of the year I had nothing to do, no income, my mother-in-law wanted some papering done and I done that for her. A lot of her friends wanted it done too. So I had about two months every spring I'd be paper hanging in Jackman. I had to be everything to get a living.

One of my uncles ran a hotel in White River Junction, Vermont, called the Adams House, and about 1931 another uncle and I leased a diner on the end of it, the Adams Quick Lunch, right near the railroad tracks. I went to White River Junction three different times during the Depression; this was the second time.

My uncle was a pretty good cook. We leased the diner for twenty-five dollars a week, and we was to furnish the lights and the gas and the coal for the big coal range there. We could seat about fourteen people at the counter and we had eight booths. Before we opened it we took two weeks to clean it up and paint it. We soaped up the windows so people couldn't see what we were doing and we went in and painted and cleaned that whole thing. We marked the soap the opening date. The night before we opened we cleaned all the soap off the windows so we'd be ready to go. We opened it in the morning and we was going to run it twenty-four hours a day. I worked pretty near all day with him that opening day, we were so busy. Then I went to bed. He come and woke me about ten o'clock and I come down and then I started to run it at night. I'd run it from six at night to six in the morning, then he would come on.

In those days it was hard times. It wasn't safe for a man to stay there alone. Good people that was hungry, I mean family people, just couldn't find work or nothing to eat. So rather than to turn them down or anything we'd go over to the suppliers and get donations of beef rack or beef bones and make a beef stew. We'd make a big wash boiler full. Keep it out in the back kitchen. They'd come to the back door.

"Well, you got to work. But you eat first, then you'll feel more like working."

Some of those fellows had gone without sleep. They'd eat and then they'd fall asleep in that heat, especially in the winter months. But we let them think that they helped us out. Of course it was always on my shift at night. I used to let them wash the dishes and kind of clean up the kitchen. But I would make them promise not to tell, to advertise it because we didn't want any more than we had to have.

A year afterwards when I was running the cocktail lounge in the hotel a man walked in all dressed up, with his wife and kid, and he'd remembered me. I had given him two or three meals. He come in and laid down a ten dollar bill that he wanted to give to me. He told his wife that this was the man that gave him meals when he was out looking. Things had changed. So it all came back. They say you get return for what you give.

I remember we used to sell an egg sandwich and a cup of coffee for a dime. Ham and egg sandwich and a cup of coffee, fifteen cents. A baked bean dinner with either yeast rolls or a couple slices of bread and a cup of coffee or tea and a brownie, a little cottage cheese for a quarter. Steak dinner, forty-five cents. Never was a dinner over fifty cents in those days. We used to buy doughnuts from a bakery there. Fellow made special doughnuts - great big ones. Doughnut and a cup of coffee for a nickel. So you can imagine how much we had to turn over to make that twenty-five dollars a week! We got our board and a salary out of it.

Then my dad died in 1932 and I went home for a while.

That's when I worked at Spencer Lake. Charlie Bratton had a set of sporting camps there and I got a job there. I was running the post office and doing chores. I used to guide some too.

In that fall, come bird hunting, Marguerite come out from Little Bigwood Lake Camps where she'd been working. I'd been courting her since we met at that dance in Jackman. We'd been pretty close and I liked her very much and she did me and so I invited her in to the Spencer Lake Camps. She come in for a week, and she shot a lot of partridge. And so while she was in there I proposed to her.

I said, "I have no ring to give you or anything now,"

I give her some money, I don't know, maybe forty dollars, fifty dollars. I says "When you go out, pick a ring of your choice, 'cause I got to keep on working." So that's the way it was left.

Then that winter I went back to White River Junction to work as night clerk and janitor at the Adams House. Fifteen dollars a week as janitor and fifteen dollars a week as night clerk.

There was quite a bit to the hotel. There was a hardware store and a pool room, bowling alley and dry cleaners. My uncle was a proud man in this way. The sidewalks had to be swept and all the rubbish from all those stores had to be put in one place. That was my job.

So I used to send my mother thirty dollars a week. First thing I know I got a letter telling me not to send any more money, that she had two or three jobs going and that I must need the money. I kept on for awhile. My uncle sent me to the National Distillers school and I learned how to be a bartender and I ran the cocktail lounge at the hotel. I brought her (Marguerite) to White River Junction too, but she didn't like the work so we quit.

Well, what started it, she couldn't get along with my aunt. So she says, "I'm going home."

I says, "If you're going home I'm going with you."

She says "You're staying here, Azel."

I says, "I'll stay one day."

Well, that wasn't much of a notice for me to give but I got out of there and we come home.

When we decided to leave White River Junction we went over to the railway station and bought tickets on a Quebec Central train that was supposed to meet a Canadian Pacific in Sherbrooke and then to Jackman. Well, Quebec Central was a little late and just as we was pulling into Sherbrooke, the Canadian Pacific was pulling out. So here we were in Canada, be another day before the train came. So I went into the Canadian Pacific ticket office, and I said, "There is something wrong. I was sold a ticket through to Jackman."

"There's nothing we can do."

"We're supposed to be in Jackman tonight."

The fellow thought a minute and he says, "I'll tell you what I can do. There's a freight up here that's coaling up. If you want to sign that if anything happens that Canadian Pacific won't be liable, you can ride in the caboose."

We signed, and when the the train came down through it didn't even stop. We boarded it still moving. The conductor and the signal man was in the caboose and they had a little fire going and whatnot and they was having their dinner. So they invited us to go up in the little cupola where we could see while they was having their dinner.

Now when you see three locomotives on steam chugging way ahead and about a hundred cars and you're winding around through the mountains and the hills through the snow...That was the most beautiful sight I think I ever saw. I enjoyed that more and I think of that now as one of the most scenic trips I ever took.

So here I am back in Maine with no job or anything.

Well, back when I worked at the Marshall House for Fred Marshall there used to be the Boundary Express went up through. The people that owned the Boundary Express, a man and his wife, had started the business together. I used to be picking up the stuff and signing for it in the afternoon because Mr. Marshall was always taking his nap. The Boundary Express was a freight outfit that became Fox and Ginn and came out of Skowhegan.

When I come back from White River the fair was on and I went down to Skowhegan. Rode down with her mother and father, sister. They turned into the fairgrounds and just about a quarter of a mile down was the car barns.

I said, "I'm going down to the Boundary Express and see about a job. I'll meet you all back here."

I went down, went into the office to talk with them.

I said, "You wouldn't have any truck driver's jobs or anything?"

"Well," he says. "Can you bookkeep?"

I says, "All depends on how hard it is. I can do it."

She says, "You've got wonderful penmanship, I know that."

I says, "When do you want me to go to work?"

She says, "Monday, at noontime. We need somebody from noon to midnight. Six days a week."

Men were working for a dollar a day. She told me, "We'll start you off at thirty-five dollars a week." Boy, I thought that was pretty good.

I said, "Would you let me have an extra week before I come to work?"

She said, "Yes, as long as we can depend on your coming."

I said, "I'll be here. I haven't even seen my family. I've just come from White River Junction. I haven't seen anybody."

I went up to the fairgrounds. She says, "When are we going to get married?"

I says, "Well, we'll have to get married in October. How's that sound to you?"

"All right."

This was the time of the bank holidays. I had had seven or eight hundred dollars in the bank but when I got it settled up I had practically nothing. But I had my job.

She told her mother. She says, "We're planning to get married in October."

I don't know if you remember the NRA, the National Relief Association. Everybody was supposed to be dedicated to help others and everything. They was having big "recovery" marches and parades all over the state of Maine. So later that fall we put some trucks in the parade from the Boundary Express. I was in the parade and I looked and there she was standing on the side of the road. Well, the parade stopped for a minute and she come out and hollered.

I said, "What are you doing down here?"

She said, "I come down to buy my wedding dress."

I says, "Oh my God! We are getting married." It was

only a week and October was going to be gone.

I says, "All right." So that night before she left to go back with her folks I told her, "I'll be up Saturday to get you."

So I went up to the office and told them. I says, "I"m getting married Saturday. I'd like to get off around four o'clock."

The lady there that owned it says, "I'll come over and take care of the work."

I bummed a Ford pick-up and I took off. I think I bought a new set of underwear, I think I had a fairly decent suit, and I went to pick her up. When I got into Jackman it was just growing dusk. Her suitcase was on the porch. I put it in the truck, got her, bid her mother and her sister and her stepfather and them goodbye. We didn't know where we was going to get married.

Got down to The Forks, to my home place, and my mother was there. I went into the house and my mother says, "What are you doing?"

I said, "I'm going to get married." I says, "She wants to change her dress."

She got all changed up and says, "Where we going to get married?"

I looked and I says, "You know, it's nine o'clock. We're going to do well if we find anybody. We might have to wait till Monday."

"Well you ain't going to sleep with me until we're married!"

That didn't give me a lot to think about. So we took off down to Bingham.

I said, "I'm going to drive in around the minister's house there to see if by any chance he might be up." His name was Arthur MacDougall. He used to be my old scoutmaster, when I was a kid.

I see the light on, stopped and went to the door. He come to the door.

"Well, Azel," he says. "What a surprise. What are you doing out this late at night?"

I says, "Reverend, I have a lady out here. I've got all my papers and everything and I'd like to get married."

"You got all your papers?"

"Yes."

"Bring her right in."

"I'm glad I didn't have to wake you," I says.

"No," he says, "I've just called a doctor for my wife." I tried to apologize and back out, but he insisted we come in.

I went out and got her and brought her in, right in his kitchen. I see another woman in there running around. He looked at the papers and everything. He went to the door and says to this lady, "Would you like to come out and witness this wedding?" She was the midwife that they had over there. She come out and she witnessed the wedding.

When the minister asked Marguerite if she would promise to take me, obey all the orders and everything, she says, "I'll try."

She didn't say "I will."

Now, this is the gospel truth. We don't know when he pronounced us man and wife if it was on the twenty-eighth or the twenty-ninth. That was fifty years ago, last year.

We went on to Skowhegan. I went to work Monday morning. We've never had a honeymoon, and this is the way our life has been, from one jump to another.

Mrs. Adams: When we were first married we'd get up in the morning and we'd have breakfast. I'd have a piece of toast and a cup of coffee and I'd give him the same. That was the first week. Then the weekend came. He got a paycheck and he says, "We're going to have more to eat for breakfast. I'm used to more and we're having more."

So he went and bought a bean pot and baked beans. I didn't know how to bake beans, Mother was a marvelous cook but she didn't teach me how. I had to learn the hard way.

The way we've always baked beans is soak them overnight. Then in the morning put them on the stove and bring them to a boil. Cook them just enough so that you take a spoonful and blow a little cool air on them, if the skin starts cracking and peeling they're good. Sometimes old beans takes more parboiling. You must test. Throw them in the bean pot. Two pounds of beans go into one bean pot. Put a few beans in, a piece of salt pork, more beans. Put an onion in and the rest of your beans, three good tablespoons of black molasses, three teaspoons of dry mustard, plenty of pepper, then fill the pot with water. We bake them in the wood stove about six hours. Keep the water to the top of the beans.

Creative Survival

When we were first married I was working at the Boundary Express as bookkeeper and I worked there for over a year. In the little office we had one of them oil stoves, the old space heaters. You set in there six days a week twelve hours a day breathing those fumes. I think I got monoxide poisoning. Along in June or July, I come down with this awful headache, dizzy. I went to see a doctor. He told me to get outside. So I went back and explained my situation to the people, the Richardsons. They were lovely people, very good.

"Well," Mr. Richardson says, "the doctor might be right. We can get along awhile. We'll find you a job outdoors."

Unbeknown to me the fellow that I was working for, Norris Richardson, contacted Roy Keene, who leased a gas station in town. He came into the office, and after a while he said "Norris has told me you're a good man, dependable. I'd like to have you tend my filling station, manage it."

I said I would.

I went down and I run this filling station. We built up a good business. We went in the tire business and whatnot and I had hired another man to help out. The owner's son ran a grocery store next door, and first thing I know he had a heart attack. So I went into the grocery store and I run that for about a year.

Then I wanted to get back home. I wasn't happy in Skowhegan. So I told the owner that I was going to take a week or two weeks' vacation. I took my wife and we moved right out of the rent we had there. Went to The

Forks. The tin shack at Durgin Corner.

There wasn't too much work right then and I left my wife and went back to Skowhegan and I went to work burnishing heels in the Somerset Shoe Shop. To let you know how unsettled I was at that time, the last day I worked I got seven dollars. The average person got two, three dollars a day. I was rugged and I set my machine up with a platform to stand on so I could use my hips to help. Instead of using just my arms and getting tired out all the time I was using my whole body. I was getting six and a half cents a case, thirty-six pairs of shoes. The last day I worked I made seven dollars and I had worked there three weeks.

I went back to The Forks and started chopping in the woods. That was when I lost the whole winter's work, didn't get paid. I'd have been in tough shape if the Fox Film Co. hadn't come along about then.

The kids find this very hard to believe, but we lived in what today you'd call a tarpaper shack. I paid five dollars a month rent. I moved in there in October, carried the water out of the brook, and every morning I'd walk two miles over the hill to meet my ride to work, then two miles into the woods and cut wood or pulp for a dollar seventy-five a cord. Walk home at night, file up a couple of buck saws so's they'd be ready to go in the morning, saw enough wood to keep her warm the next day, and green wood too. She'd put it in the oven to thaw it out a little before she put it in the stove. I worked all winter and I never saw our house in daylight. I'd leave and it would be dark and I'd come home and it would be dark. I was working for my uncle and I never got a cent of pay all winter. I never got paid period.

Mrs. Adams: I can remember, we had very little to eat - he told you that. My mother would go from Jackman to Waterville or Skowhegan. She'd come back and she'd bring us a big bag of fruit. We couldn't afford even an orange. We'd sit on this old couch, it was one that had the old horse hair and the raised head, and we'd sit and eat the oranges and the fruit that Mother had brought. You'd think that someone had given us a million. That's how appreciative we was of getting something.

We'd get up in the morning in that shack and the blanket way out around our face would be nothing but frost. If we had to go to the bathroom, if we went at night, it was in a pot. Get up in the morning and that would be frozen, just a cake of ice. I tell you...

I got beat out of my winter's wages. I was supposed to get three seventy-five a day as foreman of the crew of men cutting white birch and pulpwood down in the town of Caratunk right back of where the Sterling Hotel used to be. I was to pay my stepfather twenty five cents a day for riding. He used to pick five of us up and we'd go down to Caratunk to go to work. Along towards spring when the big cash-up was supposed to come and my uncle was supposed to pay us, he and his son and another fellow got drinking a little bit down in Bingham and they broke into two houses and stove them up. So my uncle takes the money that was to pay us which was around twenty-five hundred dollars, and used it to keep his son out of jail. So I went for the money and I got a pink slip.

Then I went to a lawyer, and it's like everything. These two lawyers got together and whoever could get the most money was the one who was going to be the winner. Well, we ended up being the loser.

Here it is April, we had nothing to eat. And because this was my grandfather's son-in-law too, my grandfather cut me off. I had no credit. Well, I'd broke my toe, and the only way of transportation was walking. From the shack we was just about two miles to Mr. Holway's grocery store at The Forks. So I went down this night, it was about six o'clock at night and it was dark, walking on my heel. I went in to see Mr. Holway.

I says, "Mr. Holway, I got to have something to eat. My wife and I." I says, "I don't know how soon I'll get back to work, you know my situation, how I got beat out."

He says, "Oh yes."

I didn't make any bones of it. I says, "My grandfather says he won't carry me. Now," I says, "I have a rifle, that's worth twenty-five or thirty dollars." I says, "I'll leave that with you as security or I'll start working tomorrow morning, anything you got to do. But I would like couple, three dollar's worth of groceries to take home."

"Well of course, Mr. Adams," he says. "Azel, what you want, you pick out."

I picked out what I needed. He turned around to me and he says, "You know, Azel," he says, "the Fox Film Company has come into The Forks and they've opened the Marshall Hotel early. Some moving picture people are coming and they are going to make a picture on the Kennebec. They must be going to hire some local help and Mr. Marshall was always your buddy. Why don't you go down and see them."

So about seven thirty I hobbled down and I went into the hotel. Mr. Marshall was at his desk, asked, "What are you doing?"

I talked for a while and I says, "They tell me there's a moving picture outfit coming to town. They going to be hiring any local help?"

He says, "I think so."

So he takes me right upstairs to Room Three and he raps on the door and gives me an introduction to this Buddy Ericson who's the director on the location. Well, this Marshall gave me quite a build-up. I didn't realize I was a good woodsman till that he told about it. So anyway, Mr. Ericson says, "Sure, come to work tomorrow morning."

I says, "What are you paying?"

"Well," he says to Mr. Marshall, "what are they getting?"

Marshall nudges me with his elbow a little bit, and he says, "Man like this, seven dollars a day. He's capable of doing everything." He says, "If I was going to hire a man I'd hire him."

"Well," he says, "Can you get some more men?"

I says, "Yes, I can find some more guides."

He says, "What do guides get?" to Mr. Marshall.

"Five dollars a day and their board. And their board is usually two dollars a day, if they board themself or if they board here."

Well, Mr. Ericson wanted us to board there. I told Marshall, "Charge for our board here."

Mr. Marshall says, "You be down here early. They won't be getting up before nine o'clock, but you fellows want to be around."

All the fellows were still up at the local grocery store talking, gassing, and when I went there to get my groceries and head home, I said, "Well, I'm going down and join the movies."

They all laughed.

Mr. Holway says, "How'd you make out?"

I says, "I got a job, seven dollars a day."

"Good, good." He reached out and he grabbed my hand and held it and says, "Thank God I let you know about it."

Well anyway, a fellow named Morris, he was there, and my brother Clyde was there and he says, "Did you get a job?"

I says, "Yeah, do you want a job?"

"Yeah. How much?"

"Five dollars a day. If you two want to go with me tomorrow morning, be right down there to sign up."

Well, my brother lived right beside the hotel so he was over at Marshall's when I got there. He says, "Was you shitting me? He said I could have a job?"

I says, "Sure."

And this Harry Morris, he walked down with me too.

When these people got moving around a little bit I took the two of them up and they were hired, five dollars a day.

They used my brother and this fellow because they were small. They were dressed up as women, curls and everything, and I took the villain's part. I was the villain and they were the girl. Stunt men, I guess you'd call us.

In the chase scene in this movie, the villain was chasing the girl through the woods on snowshoes. Then, the ice was supposed to break up along the river and the girl was supposed to jump on a cake of ice and float down the river. The movie people was there for this ice break-up. In the spring right in back of Marshall's Hotel you could look up the Dead River and see it come, so they got ready. But the ice wasn't coming, the thaw didn't come. So they wanted to speed things up.

We got about ten boxes of dynamite. We drilled holes through the ice, then tied the dynamite off with a stick across and wired it all up. We went about half a mile up the Dead River and we made artificial cakes of ice out of boards with inner tubes underneath, automobile inner tubes, to float them. We covered each "cake" with white oil cloth. We had four or five of them "ice cakes" all made and we carried them across the river to have them ready when that dynamite went off, to throw them in.

Well, this girl that I was chasing in the woods, she was there but she was over in the hotel, and the makeup men had my brother or this Harry Morris all made up. They had pictures of her running down the river bank and everything and then they wanted pictures of her jumping onto this cake of ice. They had these cakes of ice all tied together so they couldn't get too far apart. So my brother he jumped out and ran from one to the other and he lay down, and they was snapping the pictures, and here I am running along on the bank, the villain who was supposed to be chasing her.

So we went from there down the river to Solon, to the dam down by where the power plant is now. There wasn't any power plant then but there was a dam, and that was where the villain was supposed to go over the dam in a little boat. They must have bought twenty-five or thirty mackinaw frocks, and Johnson pants and fur hats and big home-gloves in the leather mitts and this was what I wore, and they dressed all these dummies up in the same outfit. They had about ten boats, little row boats that they'd bought, and they would put a dummy into a boat and put it down over the falls. They had cameras everywhere taking pictures.

They could get everything to look good right down to where the water broke over the falls. There was a sluiceway that come there and a railway bridge overhead. They put me into the boat. But they had very fine wire, they called it piano wire, hitched to the boat. There was a pier up in the river and they put a couple of men up there with a windlass to pull the boat back. In case it got stuck or anything they had a belt on me, a regular harness, and they had piano wire from the harness up to the bridge, three or four men up there pulling on that.

The men had to keep out of sight so they wouldn't be in the picture.

You know, I think they went through eight or nine boats and all those sets of clothes, new clothes. I thought that was the most disgusting thing that anybody could do. Waste? Oh!

We were down there about ten different times before they got the pictures they wanted. They'd send these pictures down to be developed and then they would say take them again. We worked there five weeks. When they got the pictures they thought they needed they paid us off and Mr. Ericson gave me a hundred dollar tip .

When I got through with the Fox Film Co. and they were about to leave Mr. Ericson called me into his room and says, "We're going to be doing a picture down on the Susquehanna River (Pa.)," and he says, "'Steamboat Round the Bend'. We can use you down there and I can get you pretty good pay as assistant cameraman working on location with us."

"Well," I says, "that's a long way from home. I'll have to talk that over with my wife."

"I'm leaving tomorrow, the next day," he says. "Come in and see me."

Well, I went up to that old tin shack we was living in. We had a couch in there and I sit down with her on the couch and we started talking it over. We talked that over and thought about it for about two hours and we decided that we'd both be pretty much out of our environment to do something like that. She says, "I don't have the clothes, Azel, to wear to go down there..." and she didn't want to go that far away from home.

So I go down and I told him. He gave me his address. He says, "If you ever want to come back to work for us, contact me and I'll find you a job." But I never went back to the movies.

So we were living in that little shack at Durgin Corner, very humble. But I paid off all the bills I owed and we had a little money left. So come summer I went to work for the state highway road commissioner in the town of West Forks, doing some repair work on the road.

Shortly after that we moved to Jackman. She went to Jackman to be with her sister who was going to have a baby. I came up after I got done on the road, but there was nothing for me to do, I had no job. Well, I happened to get talking with an old fellow who was a sport, an immigration officer, and he wanted two camps built up at Spencer Rips on the Moose River. So I took the job. I hired some men to help and we built one then. We built the other the year after.

Then I went into the lumbering business, trucking. Another fellow and I took thirteen hundred cord, if I'm not mistaken, from about twelve miles this side of the Canadian border, trucked it down to The Forks and put it into the river. Hauled six cords to a load at a dollar seventy-five per cord. I started my truck and the motor would only be shut off in the twenty-four hours to put oil in and to check it out. Run around the clock. Fifty-two miles one way and we made five trips a day. The roads and the frost started going out. I had to get this wood all into the river. There was a time limit there. I had to get it all in before the rear come down by The Forks. My last four loads I had to truck almost to Caratunk to put the logs into the river, but I got her all out.

This was in hard times. A lot of good men were loafing and what were working was getting a dollar a day. I hired an old fellow from Canada whose name was Marvel Bouchon. He was living there at the time in Jackman. I built a little camp right beside the pulp pile by the road where I'd be loading with the truck. Put a stove in it, put a bunk in it. This fellow stayed there and for twenty-five cents a load he was throwing the pulp up onto the truck so that I could pile it or my other driver could pile it up. We used to load six cord of pulp in forty, forty-five minutes. This guy used to load five loads, he was handling thirty cords a day for a dollar and a quarter. Twenty-five cents a load. If I had paid any more I wouldn't have made anything.

Along in the spring (of the following year) I bought a new truck, an International, a brand new one. Big one. I didn't really know what I was going to do with it, but I figured that there was work.

There was Valley and Valley Lumber Co. of Sherbrooke, Quebec, up at Holeb, up near the Canadian border. They had cut a million and a half feet of hardwood, yellow birch and maple eight miles back there in the woods. This fellow came down from Canada to visit.

At first I didn't know what he wanted. I didn't know quite enough French to understand. Finally I realized that he wanted me to look at that job, to truck that lumber out of the woods. This was the 24th of February. So I went out and we got the one o'clock Scoot (a train) and we went up to Holeb. We got off and we took an old Mead Morrison tractor he had and we went back into the woods eight miles.

Here we are getting to the first of March. He wanted me to truck that wood out.

I told him, "In fairness to you I don't think I should take this job. We have an early spring, we can't get it out."

He says, "How much is it going to cost?"

I says, "Ten dollars a day for the truck. I'll just furnish the truck. You pay the drivers, pay the gas and the oil and feed us. Then we got to get the road in shape."

I'd made the decision that we wouldn't load the logs on the truck. We'd just have a boom chain or something to weight the truck and we'd haul sleds like a log hauler behind. We made two roads, one iced road with ruts cut into it for both the hauling sleds and the trucks. We run what we called a rutter. It scrapes a rut in the ice just the right width for the runners of the sled and they can't leave it. The truck either. The front wheels fit in the ruts and you can go the eight miles and not even put a hand on the wheel. So we started treading the roads and running the water wagon on it and freezing it.

I took nine trucks up there the twenty-ninth of February, leap year. We landed there at night. First day of

Azel Adams and truck.

March we went off in the woods hauling. I had four crews loading trucks. We started trucking out of the woods. The twenty-fifth of March the last load of logs come out of there. A million and a half feet of wood, eight miles back in the woods to the mill at the railhead. One thing I can remember, that from the first day of March to the twenty-fifth, every morning was twenty below or colder, which was very unusual.

That was a good price, ten dollars a day for each truck. I'd hired nine trucks. I think I paid nine dollars to the other truck owners and I had a dollar bonus. We were running night and day. Never stopped.

The road we used came across a bog that they had put a lot of corduroy in and froze it in. You'd be driving along and it would be a moonlight night and you'd see these balls of fire going into the air. It was the phosphorous gases coming out of the bog. It would really scare you sometimes. Some of them would be long and tail-shape and some would be like a ball, some would be like a box or something. The trucks running over the corduroy would shake up the peat bog and release the gases. A lot of people have never seen that.

For the power to saw this lumber up they took an old railroad engine and they changed it from coal-burning over to wood. They built a concrete firebox and they burnt slabs to generate the steam for the hot pond and to run the mill.

On the brook they built a little dam and made a pond, and there was steam pipes going through the mill out to the pond. In the winter they would roll the logs into the water to get rid of the dirt and frost. It made it much easier for sawing.

We had a night watchman on then and he used to file some of the saws and he'd keep the boiler hot. We'd come in with the trucks and while they was unloading them we'd come in and get warm and probably eat a sandwich. This fellow says, "I'm awful glad you come. She's hot in here."

I says, "Hot in here?"

He says, "Yes. Haunted. I hear music."

Well, we laughed at him. One of the boys going out says, "I heard music."

So they'd listen. It was the cold wind that was blowing through that mill at night and onto those hot steam pipes that was radioing music. And nobody ever made anything of it. They'd shut up about anything like that.

So in less than thirty days from the time we put the trucks on the railroad car at Jackman we was back. Just thirty days to put a million and a half feet of hardwood lumber in the mill yard.

When I come back from that job with the Valley and Valley Lumber Company, I had my truck back home fixing it up. Another Canadian come in from up in Sherbrooke and he had two million feet of sawed hardwood lumber, all yellow birch, and it was sold to Haywood- Wakefield in Gardiner, Massachusetts, and C.F. Church Co. in Brattleboro, Vermont. He wanted it trucked from up in Canada which was forty-nine miles from my place and loaded into box cars at the rail head in Jackman.

I went over and looked at it. I said, "How much can you pay?"

He says, "Three dollars and seventy-five cents a thousand."

I said, "I can't do it for that. You make it four and I'll do it."

I had to assume the duty of seventy-five cents a thousand board feet for bringing the lumber into the United States from Canada.

So I started trucking and things was going along good.

I had a roll-off system which I started back then for loading and unloading the lumber. I had men at the mill pile the lumber onto this platform or "horse" with rollers on it and have the whole load ready. I'd back my truck underneath it and use big chain and pipe wrenches and roll it right on to my truck, throw my binder on and drive off. I had four men that I was paying sixty-six cents a day, ten hours a day. I paid their board, sixty cents a day, at the mill for to eat. They'd work ten, eleven, whatever hours they had to. I couldn't keep up with the mill so I hired a couple of trucks to haul with me.

I got it just about half hauled and the government went up another seventy-five cents duty. I told the company that I was hauling for that I couldn't stand that any more.

He said, "You've got a contract."

I said, "Yes, but it was based on what the duty was then. I didn't know and you didn't know."

He grinned and he come out with the extra duty.

Those yellow birch boards, board after board, full inch thick, not a knot in it, twenty, twenty-four foot long. A lot of that lumber was sawed up to make toilet seats by the C.F. Church & Co. in Brattleboro, Vermont, advertised the "Best seat in the house." When you stop and think what they're having to use now for furniture, and what they used then just to make toilet seats. The lovely big hardwood boards...

My wife went over with me one trip. The only trip she ever went. As I was coming out from the mill just about a mile from the mill there was a raised culvert, I went to step on it a little bit. When I did the frame broke and the truck went right up. The lumber overhung so heavy out back the truck broke right in two. I got out and looked at it. I looked and here she was coming out the door, it was way up high, and she was scrambling down. She never went again.

The competition come in on the trucking after that and things were getting worse. The government was getting into it, the ICC and all the special licenses you had to have. I wasn't getting a new dollar for an old with the truck so I decided to sell it.

We were living in Jackman when I got done trucking lumber, and some undertakers there wanted me to take a truck and haul some caskets in for them from the railhead. Well, we stopped and got a bottle of Paul Jones and we drank a little bit and we went out and got the caskets loaded.

They wanted to know what they owed me and I said, "Not a thing. I'm not doing anything."

"Well, you pull right in here." One of them reached over and grabbed the steering wheel and pulled right into the Gulf station and they wanted to put five dollars worth of gas in, which was quite a bit of gas, then.

So the fellow that owned the gas station he come out. Pumped the gas. He said, "Whatta you got there?"

"Oh we've got some caskets. Can we sell you one?"

"How much?"

I think the price was two hundred and fifty dollars.

He says, "You put me in the ground too? You put me in the casket?"

The Frenchman says, "Sure, sure. We will. You want one?"

"Why not?"

"Where do you want it?"

"Oh," he says, "put it in the back room."

So we all laughed. We carried the casket into the back room, back of the office of the filling station there and left it. He paid for it.

Well, this was a joke around town then. I heard later on, three or four months afterwards, that this fellow had shot himself. Now I think that he was thinking about that when that he bought the casket. It wasn't too much time from the time he bought the casket 'til that he'd shot himself.

I had sold my truck to pay off all of my debts and I was out of work. I did go in the woods for a week or so. I worked seven days in the woods paying my board a dollar a day. I ended up coming home with three dollars. So I decided that if I was going to starve to death I could do it right to home.

There was an advertisement that someone was going to build some cribs down on the Saco River and I heard about it, I don't know just how. So I called these people up - Greenleaf and Sons, over in Lewiston. The fellow I talked to said yes, going to start next week. Wanted to know if I'd built any cribs.

I said, "Oh yes, I built log camps, log bridges, whatnot."

But really I had not built a pier out in deep water. It was thirty-five and some odd feet deep in the Saco.

He says, "I got a fellow from your town I'm going to

call tonight. Aime Poulin, he's been a foreman for us before."

I says, "He's home."

He says, "Will you get in contact with him and tell him we want him to call?"

So I did. Aime hired out, and we took sixteen or seventeen men from the Jackman area and went down. Well, Aime went down as head foreman to start with. In a short time he made foreman on building. There was about six cribs we built at Bonny Eagle and up in Hiram Falls.

We went there in the wintertime and hauled the timbers right out on the ice. Took ice saws and cut the holes the size of the crib. Well, if you're going to build a crib and fill it with rock so that it will hold in the currents and whatnot, if you've got thirty-five feet of water it's customary to start the crib off at thirty-five feet wide. And then as you come up you make the crib smaller. We would build a floor in the crib and put ropes on all four corners. We would have the ropes anchored around with a stake froze in the ice up above and out to each side. This was so that we wouldn't be working in the water while we was building it. We'd get it up two feet high above the ice. Then we would haul rock out and load up the crib, slack off the ropes and lower it down into the water and build on to it.

I started out at sixty cents an hour and finished up at a dollar an hour and the company paid our board at a house there. It'd take ten dollars a week for seven days' board and room. We used to eat breakfast at quarter of six in the morning and eat our supper at quarter of six at night. And the lady that ran the boarding house would pack a lunch for us. Hard working men, all family men, but we went down there and we stayed until we completed the job. Then we came home.

Soon after the crib job I went to work at the Moosehead Inn in Rockwood as bartender. I'd be hired as a bartender but before I got out of there I would be in the kitchen, and everywhere to make my job secure.

At the Moosehead Inn around noontime we'd serve around a hundred dinners. At night we'd probably be down to seventy-five. Breakfast if we served twenty, twenty-five it was a good breakfast. Right around July fourth when we was busy, the salad girl who came from Bangor decided that she had to go back home to see her boy friend. Nothing I could say would keep her. She went. So I said, "Well, I'll have to do the salad."

Well, back up there in the woods everything had to come from Bangor. They was out of salad dressing. Well, I could make it with vinegar and oil. I looked and in the refrigerator there was two dozen lemons, some limes, there was a lot of green vegetables. It was getting near dinner time so I got everything else going and I decided to try to get some salad. Green peas, string beans, carrots and stuff. I grabbed the shredder and I just started shredding all that stuff and I filled a big bowl with it. Tomatoes, peppers, everything. I tossed them up. I never liked vinegar and oil. So I went and I grated some of that lemon peeling, throwed that on and tossed it in. I went and squeezed the juice out of about six lemons. I poured it all over that salad. Then I shook just enough sugar on it to take that sharp taste.

When those girls started taking the salads out with the dinners, we were serving a four and five-course meal then, everybody said, "What kind of salad is that? What do they call it?"

The girls were coming out and I was cooking meat and stuff. They asked me what I called that salad.

I said, "Oh, that's just a health salad."

Well, they wanted to know if I could tell them how to make it. You know, there was people, be up to camp somewhere else around the lake, they'd come up to the Moosehead Inn to have dinner and they'd want to know if they could have just the salad. Well, if they were just going to have the salad then I had to throw some meat in. So I'd throw a little bit of cold meat in, and cold cuts and cottage cheese. Do you know, that salad was a drawing card for the Moosehead Inn.

Marguerite was carrying Donna at the time I was working at the Moosehead Inn. When it come time and she started in with labor pains I dropped everything and I went to the hospital with her mother and her, down to Greenville. She was in there quite a little while. Well, in those days I was very dedicated to my work and I was thinking about my work and I thought that they would be depending on me and looking for me so I drove back to Rockwood. At the hospital they didn't know whether it was false alarm or what. I just got back up to Rockwood, twenty miles, and that was a rough road then, and I got a call that I had to come back. Well, I jumped into the car and away I went back.

Doc Prithim come and he says, "Look." He says, "Your wife I don't think is going to have this baby normal. She's going to have to have a Caesarean birth."

He'd already talked it over with her and she told him, "You haven't got to wait for him, it's me that needs it. Go ahead."

The doctor says, "I've done ten, maybe fifteen of these, and I've never lost a baby, never lost a woman." He says, "It's a hundred per cent for the woman, and unless the baby's dead or in trouble before, it's a hundred per cent for the baby."

So I said, "As far as I'm concerned go ahead."

So they did. The baby was born and Marguerite was sewed up. But she'd been in labor a long time and he had to make a much larger incision than normal. I went back to work pretty happy, gloating over my new baby and whatnot. Got a call the next morning around nine o'clock to come to the hospital, Mrs. Adams was very bad.

Her face was all purple, her lips, her fingers and everything and she was all bloated up with gas, pressing her heart.

I said, "Where's Doctor Prithim?"

They said, "He's gone coot hunting."

Well, I knew where he lived, and I take off. Just as I go out the hospital driveway I see his old car drive in. He got out of the car and went into his house and I followed him right in. Here he was with his hunting boots and whatnot on.

I says, "Doc, will you come up to the hospital right quick?" I says, "Mrs. Adams is in bad shape. She's all black and she's bloated up."

He reached over and picked up two raw carrots and stuck one in his pocket and chewing on the other he started over. I couldn't keep up with him. He could walk like that horse that he had. When I got up there he was in to the room where she was. He'd uncovered her and looked and her stomach was right up.

He said to the nurse, "Give me..." something. She got it. He cut the bandage down across the front, opened up two stitches and her stomach went down just like letting the air out of a balloon. Then he put on a new bandage.

He says, "She'll be all right now."

He come out and he put his hand on my back and he says, "All she needs now is rest."

He tells one of the nurses that he'd be gone a couple of hours and he takes off.

Now I'm telling you I set out in that waiting room for two hours until he come back.

I says, "Are you going in to see her?"

"Oh," he says, "She's all right, ain't she?"

I says, "I don't know. You're the one I want to look at her."

So he did. He says, "She's fine."

I go back home that night, happy.

Prohibition had been repealed some time before, but the Moosehead Inn had the only license for handling liquor in the area. I was running the cocktail lounge. The Inn owned a Cadillac, a Buick and a 1936 Ford Ranch Wagon. At that time we was handling so much liquor that when we went to Augusta to get our liquor from the liquor agency we'd take the seats out and pack the cars full. The larger percentage of it was pints, cases of pints. Used to cost right around ninety cents a pint then.

Well, one of our jobs at the Inn was to haul Golden and Laggy Labor Agency men from Bangor to St. Johns Pond up there in the woods. When you've got two or three thousand men back up there in the woods and they've all got a payroll coming in, any time a car would be going up there they'd want a bottle of liquor or so, and we was hauling men right steady.

Along the woods roads back up there they'd know when that we were coming. You'd see men standing beside the road and they'd have a little fire going there in the winter, and they'd hail us down. They'd have money for five or six men or more to buy pints. We'd never think of going up to St. John's Pond with shorter than five or ten cases of liquor. In those days you couldn't get a license to sell out like that, the only way you could sell it was by calling it "room service".

There was two bootleggers up there. One of them, she sold a lot. She sold pretty near as much as we did. But she used to get it from us. We'd go to Augusta and get a load and sell some to her. We made a little profit on it.

CHAPTER SIX

World War II to the Present

I was tending bar in Rockwood when the war (WW II) broke out. Everybody was talking about Hitler and everything and so we decided, there was three of us, that we'd better go into construction, get down on the defense. We went to Portsmouth, New Hampshire. I got hired out with Ellis C. Snodgrass down on Badger Island building the Badger Island Bridge there in Portsmouth. The other two come back to Portland and they got on something there.

After the bridge job I come to Portland and I went to the Donaldson Shipyard, building launching ways, still working for Ellis C. Snodgrass.

Then we started the West Shipyard and this was when I learned to dive. This fellow I was working for, Bob Rabbit, he was a diver. He was superintendent later for Ellis Snodgrass. He was a man that weighed around three hundred and twenty-five or so, six foot six. He wore a number six diver's suit, the biggest they made and that was really too tight for him. I was tending him one day and he was getting tired.

He says, "I'm not going back down. It's two hours' work and I'm just not going to do it."

"Well," I says, "if it's only two hours work, can't I do it?"

He says, "Sure. That suit's going to be pretty big for you."

Three or four of us was on the rig, and they were laughing. I got into the suit, put the shoes on. I couldn't have carried the lead that he had. He had about a hundred pounds of lead on his belt. Anyway I went down. It was only about eight feet of water, just over my head.

We was cutting off pilings, had three pilings to cut off. I used to look at him, 'course he came from out around Michigan way, and I'd look at him and he'd be upright and he'd squat down and take hold of this saw and he was going back and forth with it. Well, being a woodsman, I would bend right over and saw with my head down. So I was going to show him how to saw that tree down, that piling.

First thing I knew that air coming into my helmet crawled up my back and was in the seat of my pants and up my legs and I was standing up. I was on my head and my feet up and I couldn't get righted up. You can't either. And how them fellows laughed and they let me float around like that for a while before they straightened me out. But I learned. I learned that I could step up to a pile and cut it off right but I had to have a tight belt around my waist to stop the air.

In the West Yard we had a lot of piling to cut off. At one time I think we had about ten divers working in the fortification of Casco Bay, building cribs and whatnot. I had the charge of a diving crew a little while. Had a couple of divers aboard a rig and we had a little house built right on the diving rig and in a short time I seemed to become the foreman for diving. I had some good divers working for me there. I ended up getting myself a number two suit and a helmet. I had my own outfit. I didn't use it much, but I'd have it aboard. When I left I sold it and I've been sorry ever since. I had bought the suit for sixty dollars and I bought a three-cylinder compressor, a lot of weights and a lot of equipment. I sold the whole works for fifty dollars. Right now that whole outfit would be worth a thousand.

We got a lighter (a barge) from up in Eastport. It had been bought in 1931 to be used up in Quoddy Head when they was going to start that power plant. The government had scrapped the idea and that lighter was on mud flats up there for about ten years. By 1942, the people in Portland was looking for anything that would float. So Leonard Arsenault took four or five of us and we caulked that thing up and got it in shape, pumped it out and got it towed to Portland Harbor. Sanders Engineering used it one winter before it was returned to Ellis Snodgrass. We done some repair work on the booms and the boilers, and the swing engines and the hoisting engines was all gone over.

So I started with that lighter around the Portland Harbor, going wherever the navy needed work to be done. The navy wanted to put in a big underground battery of guns on Diamond Island at the mouth of the harbor. Lane Construction Co. had the contract to do that so they hired the lighter and Snodgrass sent me and the operator and the fireman with it. There was three of us went with it.

We were hauling reinforcing cement, gravel, sand, and all the equipment, cranes and everything, out to the island. We worked there for four or five months. When we got done with Lane we took the lighter over to Long Island building docks there.

They was bringing piling to the Atlantic coast from the Pacific coast by railroad. The railroad yards used to run beside Back Bay near Forest Avenue clear to Burnham and Morrill's. There was a bridge at Burnham and Morrill's, and the railroad track used to run right down underneath that. They used to bring the piling in and unload it there. These pilings ran anywhere from seventy feet to a hundred twenty feet long. The long ones would be on three flat cars.

We was getting a few pilings for the Long Island dock. First thing I know this became the staging area for the whole Atlantic seaboard, and I had to gear up and start making up shipments of piling. Unload and reload cars with piling of different lengths for Davisville, Rhode Island, or Massachusetts or wherever they wanted it. Before we finished we was even sending out to the Mediterranean.

Pilings from the Pacific coast.

At the same time we were putting in degaussing ranges out from Fort Preble to fortify the harbor. This was underwater piling that was sawed off twenty-five feet below the high tide level. Things that seemed like big brass kettles were put on the pilings to sense any boats coming in or out. Just above that there was a line of torpedoes that could be set off from shore. They drove pilings, sunk old ships between the islands so that the U-boats couldn't get in.

Finally we took the lighter and went down to help finish up the docks on Long Island. I moved my wife out there (to Long Island), and they gave me one of the best houses on the island. It was right directly back of the office and free rent, but I was married to that job twenty-four hours a day. Just as soon as V-E day came and I had a little time of, and I said, "Let's go in town."

I heard about the Maine Turnpike going to start, and Lane Construction Co. had the contract. Lane Construction Co. was the company that I'd worked for transporting the stuff out to Diamond Island. So I had worked with the superintendent, I had more or less proven myself to him, and I went in to see him.

He said, "Just the man I want. Going to need somebody cutting right of way from here to Portsmouth."

He didn't give me much chance to work a notice but I got offen that island. I went to work before I got my wife moved off. I had so much compensatory time built up that I come offen there in May and went to work for Lane Construction Co. and I didn't get my last check from the United States government until in November. And I got a raise in that time.

After the Turnpike job wound down I went to work on the Union Falls Dam on the Saco River. I was running the gun on the second shift, nights, and we was building the coffer dam.

I see that the work was coming so much that I suggested that they put a third shift on. We was working seven days a week and that was too much. So the supervisor left it to me to set up a third shift, and the guy I picked to run the gun on the third shift was the supervisor's cousin. I didn't know it at the time, but they didn't speak! They didn't get along. But he did do a good job.

We had a flood go through there in the wintertime. We had the coffer built, and all the stuff down in the hole, and we got word from up around Hiram that the Hiram dam had broke loose and to expect about five or six feet of water. We only had about two foot freeboard right then. I got the word about six o'clock at night and that water would be down there in about four hours.

Well, we had some crib work that we were building and they'd brought in some new timbers. I got every man offen their jobs and down in the hole, the carpenters and everything, and I got a cherry picker. I didn't have an operator to run it so I run it myself. We got them timbers up and stacked them one on top of another, building up that coffer dam. By the time we got one row of logs clear across, the water was lapping right at the bottom of the timbers. And we'd put another row. We'd put oakum in between and we'd spike the timbers down so that they would hold. We had knee braces in to hold them from tipping over. We used every log that we had. I said, "Now if she goes over, she goes over. We've got nothing else to put on."

The water made its crest right there and it was halfway up on the last log across. The machinery, equipment that was down in that coffer, a hundred thousand dollars, two hundred wouldn't pay for it. But we saved it. The water went down.

We always loved to dance.

Back in Jackman, that first night we met, when that she picked me for her partner there, Willie Fournier didn't like that too well. He was a wonderful dancer. He could really dance, but for some reason she picked me that night. There was that contest for the best dancers. If I had dared to drink I think we could have won.

Boy, we used to polka a lot. We would polka for an hour. This was in later years. I was on to construction in Connecticut. I had a brother down in Washington, D.C. So come Memorial time instead of coming north, we went down there to visit his family. We met up with a cop that was originally from Maine and his wife. Nothing to do but that they took us down to the Dixie Wheel, a lounge and dance hall. Well, her and I, we kept after this old colored guy that was playing the piano to play the polka. We started dancing polka. Well, everybody stopped and watched us when we was doing our polka. We thought nothing of it. First thing you know the old colored guy says, "Don't hurry. We keep going. We're going to keep going."

But we had to move because the Dixie Wheel closed at 12 o'clock at night.

He called this gambling joint, the Jester Club, and asked permission to bring our party down. We didn't know anything about the place. So we got down there. It was all gamblers. You could buy a bottle there and have it brought to the table and everything. The old colored guy come in and started playing. We wasn't in any hurry to get up dancing, so finally he says, "You got to get up and dance. I'm going to play this polka for you."

So he played the piano and we got up and danced. All of them guys came out from the back room, them gamblers, and watching us and clapping their hands, just to see us polka. We didn't realize that we was the entertainment. I'm not bragging, but we could step it out. Lawrence Welk, he don't move fast enough for me. When we'd polka we was doing it fast. A few automobile accidents, a little age took that all away.

I'd like to live that life over just for the dances. When we were in Portland, I was working six, seven days a week twelve hours a day during the war. I'd come home Saturday night, "Going to a dance," and we'd go.

We'd eat in a restaurant. We'd go up to North Windham and come home two, three o'clock in the morning and I'd have to go to work at six. Now I'm telling you Sunday was a long long day.

We used to go out to Oak Hill in Scarborough. Then we started going to the Falmouth Grange Hall. We got to know everybody. The last time we went there, an old buddy of ours dropped dead right beside of her feet, had a heart attack. It was during the last dance and our friends had gone and sat down. When we came around, I jokingly said, "What's the matter. Couldn't you take it?"

So we kept dancing around. Finally they got up again and danced a little while and the dance stopped. We all went and sat down and our friend sat down and fell. Never breathed again. After they got him out they started the music again. Marguerite got up and she says, "I've heard everything. I'll dance at your wedding but not at your funeral. Let's get out of here."

So we went home. I don't think we've been dancing since then.

I was at Union Falls, Maine, for about four years. Then I went from that job to Wilder, Vermont. In fact a lot of the equipment we used building the dam at Union Falls was sold to the New England Power Co. in New Hampshire. I was up there over four years. I stayed after everybody else.

(The Wilder Dam is on the Connecticut River, just north of Hanover, N.H., and White River Junction, Vt.)

On the Wilder Dam there when we cleaned up the bottom of the river we found a lot of antique artifacts. We found some muskets, some guns with just the metal parts left and they claimed that they was from Roger's Rangers, that he'd lost a lot of men in those falls there. We found a lot of antique handmade axes, saws, cant dogs, and stuff that had come down the river.

When we started the Wilder Dam, we started on the New Hampshire side preparing the base of the dam to receive the concrete and make sure it was all solid. One of the first things we found when we got a road down in there was a set of locks. There was two locks that we could see that had been used to bring boats up. They was laid up out of field stone and cement. Just side of us there was a road that had been built up through to Dartmouth College in Hanover. When they enlarged the road they either buried or took out another lock, because I know that there had to be another lock in order to get up around the falls. There was oak trees a foot, two foot on the butt growing right in them locks, so you see how long they had been there.

A little closer to the river there was a railroad track. We begin to ask questions about that. Come to find out, after the time of the locks they put in a narrow-gauge railroad. Boats would come up as far as the locks, they'd load stuff onto the railroad. They'd haul the freight beyond the falls with horses and then load it back into boats and go clear up to Orford, New Hampshire.

We built a coffer dam on the main part of the river where the main dam and power house was supposed to be, and the coffer dam pushed the water over on the Vermont side. I went on nights then, running the job nights. The whole base of that river across there was full of potholes. They could be no more than a foot across or they could be five or six feet. The base of that river was just as hard a fine-grain granite as you ever could ask, but the site of the new dam was right to the bottom of a set of falls. The water coming down would dump rocks over that falls and the current would start spinning the rocks. It would grind these potholes out just as smooth as could be. Some of them would be three or four feet deep, some about six inches deep. We struck one pothole over on the New Hampshire side that was about eight, nine feet across at the top.We went down twenty feet, shoveling it out and it took a couple of nights doing it. When we got to the bottom there was a rock in there just about the size of a basketball and just as round and smooth as it could be. And the bottom of the hole was just round and smooth. We couldn't have built anything that would be any better for the bottom of that dam than those holes. We'd stick rods of iron down in there and then we'd pour concrete around them and they never could move or slide.

It was just above that on the Vermont side that we drilled down and we dropped into that underground river.

On those hydro jobs we always had a mineralogist, a guy that was sent in by the government to approve all the river bed before we put down any concrete. Well, this fellow's name was Crosby and I had worked with him before.

So I said, "What are we going to do on this bottom? Are we going to clean her right down like we did on the other job?"

Normally test bores would be made before the dam was built to determine the nature of the base of the dam.

"Well," he said, "if we've got any potholes we've got to trace them out, you know that. But I've got a little different method so as not to slow us down and I think it will work as good."

I says, "What'll that be?"

"Well," he says, "we're going to run grout pipes right up through the dam. As we come up in the layers of concrete we'll have this two-inch pipe run right straight up. But it's got to be kept perfectly straight and plumb so that we can put the boring steel and core drill down into the ledge below it. Then we'll grout it."

I said, "That sounds like a much simpler way, but it's going to take a lot of pipe."

Grouting means that they mix up a hi-early cement. Hi-early means it sets up fast, and they mix it with just water and a little bit of sand. They don't mix it in a cement mixer, it's like a puddling machine. Then they just pump it into the hole, and it will go down and fall into all the seams.

So after the dam was all built and it was in operation I was in there with a crew of men cleaning up. Everybody else was laid off. All these pipes was sticking up level with a plug in them. I had a crew on top of the dam set up to go right straight across. They'd set the core drilling machines up over the holes, run the rods down till they hit bottom and then they'd screw another five-foot section of rod. Then they'd start core drilling. They was using diamond drills. They'd take a core out and while they was core drilling this Mr. Crosby'd check it. He'd tell us if we had to grout or not , and how much, when.

They pulled one core out, I know, I marked right where it was on that dam - the third lift from the Vermont side - and they pulled up a core there that had over twelve inches of gold and it looked like silver, but it was gold. There was a lot of hush on that and so I asked a fellow about it later. I think it was one of the New England Power men.

I says, "What'll they do with that?"

He says, "Well, that's going to a museum, probably up in Hanover."

I never checked. I doubt if it ever...That gold that was in that core was a foot long and two inches in diameter and it was a good yellow.

We went along, and first thing I knew one of the boys said to me, "Lost a drill."

"What do you mean?"

He said, "When I unscrewed it, it dropped."

I said, "How far did it drop?"

"About seven feet." This meant that there was a hole about seven feet deep that had no dirt or anything.

I said, "Are you going to be able to get on to the drill?"

"I'll put three or four sections of rod together and reach down and try to screw it in."

First time he done it he got it. We called Crosby. They'd take the cores out of the inside of the drill and they'd put them in a box in trays we had and they'd mark the feet, the depth of each core. So here we had about seven feet with nothing but a hole down there. So what were we going to do?

Crosby says, "Put some dye down."

So we put some dye in some water and pumped a lot down and then we went down on the river bank to see where it come out. About a hundred and fifty feet below the dam we could see this dye coming out on the side. We pumped about a hundred bags of grout in and let it set overnight.

The next day we put some more dye in to see where it come out. You'd have to see where the dam is and where the town of Wilder is, because you wouldn't think that this could happen. The town is over two hundred feet higher than where we were down at the dam. That night at the little store there in Wilder where I often stopped to pick up cigarettes or whatever, I heard a woman say, "Is your water green?"

"Yes, my water is green."

Every well in the town of Wilder was turned green. I didn't say a word. I went down to the office and I got on the telephone and I called the New England Power Co., and I told them about it. I called our company and I told them about it.

"Don't do anything, don't say anything, we'll be there in short order."

By eight o'clock at night they had all landed. So we went up into the town and told the residents that the water was not poisoned and it was just a coloring, and that we had intercepted the same stream that their wells was on.

Crosby claimed that that was an underground river and all those wells was tapped into that underground vein.

We put in about five carloads of cement down two two-inch holes, just kept mixing and dumping, mixing and dumping, until we sealed off all of the wells. We sealed everything off. We had to run a pipeline up from White River Junction to get the people of Wilder some water. But the town of White River didn't have water enough to supply them.

Finally Crosby come down and starts riding around.

I thought he was crazy, that things was getting to him. We furnished him with a little Jeep to run around in. He was all over the side hills.

He come back in the office one day and he says to me, "I've found some water."

I says, "You have? Where?"

He says, "Right up in the airport. There's a nice vein of water about fifty feet underground."

Here was the airport about three hundred feet higher than the town of White River and here was a river running underneath the airport. How this old timer knew I don't know. But we got hold of the town manager of the town of White River and Mr. Crosby told him, "You drill right here."

He walked out between the N-S and E-W runways.

He says, "You want to be drilling with a sleeve, because it's artesian and under pressure. You want to drill a ten-inch hole. Be sure and drill through a valve that you can close off, because when you bust into that river you're going to have pressure."

Having said that he left them.

The town hired an outfit from Windsor, Vermont, to go up there and drill and when they did they drilled with a sleeve but they wasn't drilling through a valve. The town of White River is terraced around the hill and when they hit water there was a gusher coming right down over the hill. I'm telling you it was some time getting it plugged.

White River Junction was getting water prior to that out of White River itself. Now they have beautiful spring water piped in by the New England Power Co. And Wilder does too.

There was a dam above the site of the new Wilder dam that had been built in 1927. Well, before we could flood the new dam, close the gates and flood it, they told me that I'd have to get a crew in there and dynamite the old one. I had visited my cousins there when the old dam was being built.

I sent a big crew of men up there, ten or fifteen of them, drilling anywhere they could get a hole in that concrete. Well, I thought I had it so there'd be no problem at all at flattening that dam. And everybody else did too. We loaded it up and we had about a ton and a half of dynamite, we used sixty per cent powder and we set her all off to once. When we set that off I said, "She'll be just like crushed gravel down at the bottom of the river."

Well, all those holes that we had down there, wherever the drill went down we put the dynamite there. Should have put the dynamite the full length of the hole. But two sticks in a four foot hole was about all you'd use, or if it were a ten foot hole you'd use three or four. What happened, instead of just exploding all the concrete she just blew potholes out the side of the dam. And there it stood after that dynamite went off, the worst looking mess, a bunch of reinforcing steel holding a bunch of concrete up in the air. We had to start with burning torches, paving breakers. I worked three months with a crew of twenty, twenty-five men, night and day to get that dam out of there. And we thought it was going to be so easy. We found there was railroad iron and everything stuck in that old dam for reinforcing, and that wasn't about to blow too easy. That was about the worst experience of my life. It was a learning experience, I'm telling you.

So when we got the old dam all blown out and the river all drained down, here was another wooden dam that was built back in the eighteen hundreds for lumbering. I looked it over and that lumber was just as solid as it was the day it was built, except for some of the boards that was exposed through the years. So the company said I had to take that dam out too.

I put a big fifty-ton crane on each side and walked them on timbers right out into the middle and I started ripping it out. There was pine and spruce logs forty and sixty feet long, that's the way they was cut. And they was hand-hewed on two sides, the bark was left right on them. They was fastened into the dam with hardwood pins with inch-and-a-half, two-inch holes driven where they'd have a cross tie. These checks was ten foot apart. So every ten feet on these logs would be two inch-and-a-half holes. There was no nails, nothing in them. We was using a grapple hook and clamshell and they'd reach out to pick them logs up and they'd start to yank and yank and they'd almost tip the crane over.

They was breaking this lumber, and I looked at it and I said, "Gee, it's too bad to break that."

So I had a phone to each side so I told the operators to try to pull them out, lift a little there, come back in, lift a little, save them logs. Well, they tried it.

I went back down to the shop and I got hold of an electric generator and I brought it up and a big 3/4 electric auger with an inch-and-a-half auger in it to bore them pins out. We saved every one of them logs. 'Course I'd have to burn them or haul them off, so I contacted Trumbull's Mill over in Wilder, Vermont.

"Oh, I don't think they're worth anything."

"Well," I says, " We'll bring a load and you open it up and see what this is."

There would be pine boards there two foot across, just as clear as they could be, but when they dried out they turned a little yellow. But that pine today would be worth so much! They took them, but we had to load it for them. I dare say that there was five hundred thousand feet of lumber there.

We got that wooden dam just about cleared out and a flood come on. This heavy rain come and it rained for three or four days and finally it ended up a regular hurricane, a lot of water. So the trees along the bank of the flowage of this old dam begin to slide into the river and they piled it up right where the old wood dam had been. We was right in there again with the clamshells and bulldozers cleaning it out.

I worked about a year after the dam was completed and all I was doing was dealing with problems that the designers of the dam didn't expect.

While we were building that dam, housing was very hard to get. All of the men that was over there, even to the head superintendent, all come from Maine. But we had no place to stay, no place to bring our families over.

Finally I got acquainted enough to see that there was part of a village, they called it East Wilder, which was not going to be flooded right away but which the power company had bought. Eventually the water would be up into the cellars of these properties so the company had bought the whole thing. When I began to look everything over on the plans these houses were going to be demolished. So I nailed the superintendent and he went to the power company and they said sure we could stay there. No rent or anything.

We were the first to move in, my wife and I and kids, and there were seven houses in there and they was all people from Maine, so they nicknamed this town, we lived there three years, Mainiac Village. It was a dead end street. Any occasion could happen it would be a party. It wouldn't take too much what that we would have a party. We had a victrola, we'd carry that right out on the lawn, put a strings of lights up. We'd have chicken feeds, venison steak feeds... what times we had there! The very best of living.

I was able to go anywhere and get a job. That was it. I was never refused. I was fired once in my life, the rest of the time I quit. Until I went on construction there was no jobs that was long term. On construction I hit several jobs that lasted three or four years. I was on the Wilder

Dam in Vermont for about four years. Then I worked on the power plant in Wiscasset, Maine. We moved to Richmond at that time, and we lived there two to three years.

After I finished at Wiscasset I went down to build the docks and tank farm down to Harpswell. I worked there pretty near a year. Then this superintendent I was with in Wiscasset who had gone back to work with United Engineers on the Housatonic River in Connecticut, he called one day and asked me to go down there and work with him.

"Well," I said, "I've got a beautiful job here, and I'm being paid good."

"How much are they paying you?"

"I'm getting about a hundred and twenty-five a week."

"I'll give you two hundred and twenty-five. Four years work."

I come home and talked with her. I gave my notice, two weeks. The man that owned the company was down in Florida. He come back my last day and he found out I was leaving. He said, "Why did you decide to move?"

I said, "Money."

He said, "How much are you getting?"

I told him.

He said, "I'll pay that."

I said, "I've already committed myself. I tried to do business with the office but the project managers wouldn't recognize the need."

So when I left he promised me that if anything ever

Shepaug Hydroelectric Development. Housatonic Rive Connecticut.

happened to come back and see him.

I went down to Connecticut and I stayed four years, a little more. I come back and hadn't been back home more than four or five days when I met an old friend and he told me he had a job for me up in Aroostook County putting in NIKE bases.

We built them in about a year and a half, two years, and it was about a five million dollar job. Built one base in the town of Caribou, one in Fort Fairfield, one in the town of Connors and one in Caswell. The air base was right there in Limestone, and these NIKE bases was set off at four points of the compass within five, ten miles of that airbase. And they had all these underground missiles and everything, but they never loaded a missile, they never put a warhead in there. The bases was obsolete, the government said, by the time we got them built.

After that I went to the Narraguagus and built the flood control dam for the army engineers right at the Stillwater Pool, the famous salmon pool, near Cherryfield. Just got that completed and I went for Stone and Webster up in Woodland, I put in the digesters and the pulp room and storage railroad tracks. I went to Bar Harbor and built the Jackson Lab and the ferry terminal and the double decker motel by the ferry terminal and three miles of road up over Champlain Mountain. I was general foreman or supervisor for all of these jobs.

If you've been to Bar Harbor as you drive back of the Jackson Lab and you take that road up over Champlain Mountain down to Ocean Drive, that was the road. All that stone masonry that make those bridges, the big cut granite and beautiful stone arches. I'd never done that before but I was oh, so fortunate. So fortunate!

I had time before I did the stonemasonry and everything to get acquainted, to find out what I was going to do next, how to do it. I found some old stone cutters from up in Franklin, Maine, and I found an old quarry man and a master stonemason. They weren't working, so times had grown hard for them. I was very fortunate to get those men. I just told them what I had to have. They couldn't read the plans, but I'd tell them and they'd do it. Very dedicated. Them arched bridges, keystone arches...

That's where I was working when I got stove up.

I was laid up about two years. I got a plastic knee. I was driving a '61 Ford in that accident.

It was on a Saturday morning, raining hard, and I left a note in my office "Raining too hard. I've gone to Portland. You fellows go out and get your deer." and I left there to come home. It was November 22, and I was coming home to close on a house here in Richmond.

I come down into the town of Liberty and it was just getting daylight and they was having a hunters' breakfast. "Well, what's any better than having a good breakfast?"

I had stopped and relieved myself at the side of the road. I looked up on the side hill and I see a hunter going up there. I got in the car, lit a cigarette, got my gun, laid it beside of me, jacked it open, two shells in my shirt pocket in case a deer come out. I drove just about fifty feet and here was this car coming at me, I dare say sixty anyway, and he was looking at this lady passing. This is how plain I could see. I hit my horn and I pulled on the wheel but he hit me right on the front. Put that wheel right up into the cab with me. My head went through the window. The seat come ahead and cut my foot pretty near off, and the emergency brake handle buried right through my knee. I couldn't feel anything wrong. Wasn't I bleeding! My nose was busted and my jaw. An eight-inch piece of the horn ring broke off and just missed a main artery at my heart and went through to my shoulder blade. I didn't know I was hurting. They got me to the hospital, patched me up.

And that company I was working with dropped me like a hot potato. I didn't even get a get-well card from them. One or two of the fellows that took my place at work, they come in. There was no insurance. Rough, rough.

So, she had to go to work, while I laid here in this house. I got a plastic knee and I was laid up about two years.

I was setting in here I see an ad wanting a salesman for Hasco Manufacturing Co. I had an old high drive Plymouth. My leg was in a cast and I went out and crawled into that. I had taken her to work down here at the shoe shop. I took off for Westbrook. I went in there on crutches, and Harris Small come out from the back office. He looked, and he kept looking at me.

I said, "Yes, you know me." I remembered that we had worked together during the War.

We got talking and I told him what happened to me. "Well," he said. "What can I do for you?"

I said, "I see you had an ad selling windows, doors, siding, whatnot." I said, "I didn't know whether I'd be able to do it or not, but I sure as hell would like to try."

He said, "I don't see why not."

So he went and got his head salesman, told him to fit me all out with everything and give me a briefing. I stayed there just about an hour, and I took off. I got home at three o'clock, or three thirty and she was mad. I hadn't told her where I was going and I was late picking her up.

I took the car and the briefcases and stuff they'd given me and I started to ride around town. I went over on a back street here and a Russian had bought an old house, ironically, the house that I was going to buy when I left Bar Harbor. The windows were all broke. He couldn't talk English and I couldn't talk Russian, but I sold him four hundred dollars' worth of windows and doors and called the company that night. They had them up here the next day and put them in, and brought me my bonus of sixty-five dollars.

I went on from there selling. I should never have gone back on construction, but I did. I was building the interstate around Bangor a few years later. Four million dollar job. Three, four bridges in there in three miles of interstate. Thirty-two houses to move. I took that job and I thought they was foolish to even think of taking me back.

I had gone ten, twelve thousand dollars in debt, with all my hospital bills, mortgage on the home and all. So I started advertising in the Kennebec Journal, "Free estimates for siding, windows, doors, all building materials." I got hold of a woman who had an answering service to take the calls during the day. I had it understood that anything way out of town that I couldn't take care of evenings, I'd take Saturday and Sunday. You know that Kennebec Journal covered the whole northern part of Maine. I was getting calls from Fort Kent, Caribou, Hainesville, even New Brunswick. When I got ready to pay my income tax that year the IRS questioned it.

They come to check my income tax because I made more money selling for Hasco Manufacturing Co. than I did as superintendent on the construction. I used a Mercury Turnpike Cruiser for travelling sales and I had my own pickup that I used for the construction company. I was putting in about eighty hours a week. But I made back what I'd lost. I didn't get all my health back, though.

I recall one day I'd packed up in the morning and went to rap on a few doors. So here I am, leg in a cast, and I was trying to sell. I went into Belfast and I see this great big house there loaded with windows. Big apartment house. I went along and I got my bag and my crutches and everything and I walked to the house and rapped on the door. A woman answers it and I asks her if she was the landlady.

She says, "No."

She slammed the door awful quick. When I got out of the car with all them crutches and everything I wasn't going to give up. She didn't even last long enough for me to find out who to talk to. So I see a walk going around the building and I went around back and I rapped on the door and the same woman answered. She said, "What's this? Did you think you'd have better luck at the back door?"

"Well," I said, "most generally they're a little more congenial."

She looked at the situation. She says, "The landlord will be here in a short time, if you want to you come on in and sit down. He'll be collecting rent. Will you have a cup of coffee?"

Started talking with her. Wasn't long this man drove up in a Cadillac car.

She said, "There's a gentleman here that would like to see you."

So I got talking with him. I told him I represented the Hasco Manufacturing Co. out of Westbrook, and I told him I knowed he didn't have any combination windows on and asked him if he heated the building or his rentors did. He said that he furnished the heat. Then I give him the pitch that I could save him enough in four years to pay for the windows, and then it would be gravy from then on.

The company sold ten windows and a door for two hundred and fifty dollars, all installed. Then they had a free canopy to go over a door that the salesman could give away. I started counting the windows.

There was sixty-four windows and twelve doors for that apartment house. So I gave him the price.

He says, "What's the terms on that?"

I said, "We can finance it. You'll have the finance charges and the interest and whatnot but I'll..."

He says, "Do you want the check now?"

I says, "No, not until they're installed. You look them all over, then you pay. You don't pay me, you pay the installer."

I just happened to be there the day the windows were

delivered and I hung around while they were being installed. You're there doing that. Some other people looking, they ask the installers, and the installers say, "The salesman's right around here. He'll take care of you."

Anyway I sold enough that winter that I became the top salesman out of thirty-two that they had and they give me free TV advertising. That's when TV's first come out and I done awful good selling, but I went back into construction.

Mrs. Adams: We did a lot of moving. It just seemed every place we ever went to, I'd hardly get in and get the place cleaned for us to sit down to a table and eat and the bathroom so you could use it when he'd come home with four men behind him. They were going to board and room with us. And this is the way every job went. I never worked out, but I did get boarders.

We moved to Salem, New Jersey, in the late 1960's. You remember that was the time of all the riots. Our landlady scared me half to death. She was a very religious person and she used to go to church real often. She'd park where she could dart right into the church because she was afraid and she got me so I was scared to death to even go out into the yard. I didn't like it down there at all.

Mr. Adams: I didn't see anything wrong all the time I was in Salem. I had three hundred men in one department and they was all colored but four. The other ones were halfbreeds. I had probably two hundred and fifty in the pile-driving force, half of them were colored. Iron workers, there were very few colored. In the teamsters, about fifty-fifty. I had thirty-five hundred men on that job when I quit.

We were building a nuclear plant, power plant. To go down there as civil superintendent with only a high school education, with thirty-five hundred men working for me... If anyone had told me this would happen in anybody else's life I wouldn't believe it.

The job was on an island seven miles out in the bay, and when I started there were only a few men working, surveying and getting ready to put in well points and to make the land stable. No road out there yet.

I was watching the jobber building the road and the bridge out there and getting nowhere. The men were going by ferry boat to the island and then trying everything to get around on the island, overland sprites and things that go on land and water. It was all costing money. We was hiring more and more men. As we headed up to about two hundred men working twelve-hour days, two shifts, I thought there was no way this would ever do.

I was home one Sunday and I was setting on the porch and I see a helicopter going by. I begin to think. I said, "I bet I can transport men back and forth by helicopter cheaper than I can by ferry. Paying these men for riding the ferry and time and a half and double time, some of them get ten dollars an hour."

I called the Keystone Helicopter Co. that Sunday and

Creative Survival

got the head of the company down there. He landed a helicopter in my back yard. I had to put a sheet out there to show him where I was. He picked me up, took me out onto the island from the mainland, talked it over. He timed himself back and forth, told me what he'd have to have. By putting five helicopters down there he would be able to transport three hundred and fifty men in a half hour. He'd start at five thirty in the morning. It would take him just about half to three quarters of an hour to make a complete shift change.

I brought all these statistics into a meeting, told my company what I had done. They thought it was wonderful, if I could get the trades to go along with my plan. So we had to call a meeting with the trades. They decided they would. I was surprised.

To get my work done, to get around, to cover the job and everything, we had no roads that we could travel on, we kept a Bell helicopter during the day. And that meant we had a helicopter on the island during the day in case of accident, for evacuation to the hospital in Salem. Having this helicopter on the island in case of accident was the big reason the trades went along with the deal.

It cost sixty thousand dollars a month, when we only had a small crew. When we was going by ferry, we paid a hundred and eight thousand dollars.

We had hard luck. When the bridge out to the island was completed, then they had built the road, five miles of road over this peat bog. They had the road all built so that they was driving over it. I went down one morning, we'd had a big rain, like a hurricane in there, and about a quarter of a mile of that road had just settled right down, and out on the sides the peat just rose right up. We had to get the helicopters back. We'd only had them off about two days. It took about three months to get that road to where it would hold again.

There is a grass called phragmites. There they call it foxtail. It grows about fourteen foot tall, and the stem might be about as big around as my thumb. It was ringed like bamboo, and all that would be on it is just that brush on the top. That whole island was covered with it. The geese come in there and the birds, never see anything like it in the fall of the year. I don't know if they was feeding on them foxtails or not, but they told me that five years prior to my being down there on that island that they didn't have any foxtails, but they was very abundant down in North Carolina. They'd had a hurricane that blew all of them seeds up north and the island just became infested with them.

I left the island. I didn't stay for the completion of that job. I knew the same company had a job in New England, and my wife had gone back to Maine and it was no way for me to live. I told the company that they could transfer me or that I would leave. So they transferred me up here to Newington, New Hampshire, to start a job on a power plant. It was a fossil plant, 500 megawatts. That was the last job that I done. They forced us to retire at sixty-five and I had five months vacation due, and between our sickness and generally falling apart...

194   Creative Survival

When I got to Newington, I got to be safety engineer. I prided myself that for about twenty-five years I hadn't had a man killed by accident, but on that job I had three men drop dead by heart attacks. The last job I run. One truck driver and two hoisting engineers, and they all happened in the morning before the men went to work. They'd just got in, and before they went on the job.

The hoisting engineer, he was getting old and if I see him I usually gave him a ride down to his crane. He told me not to pick him up any more.

I said, "Why?"

He said, "The rest of the fellows think that I'm hob-nobbing with the boss."

I said, "That's too damn bad. When we get this age if we can help each other out, we're going to do it."

"No," he says. "I'm all right and I'm going to walk."

He went down, talked to his son awhile - they owned the machine - got up to walk over to his rig and he fell over.

That was in the early seventies.

When I finished that job with United Engineers I was sixty-one, sixty-two. I had five months vacation built up so when we completed the job I was going to take three months and then get reassigned. At the end of the three months she had her first heart attack. Well, I could have gone to Caracas, Venezuela, but I'd have to commit myself for seven years. I told them I couldn't do that. I ran out my vacation, took a leave of absence. They wanted me to go to Petersburg, Virginia. I couldn't go. Then they come out with the law that anybody who was sixty-five was to be laid off. So I was sixty-three, and in the meantime I was selling here to make both ends meet.

So then we both decided to retire. We retired as of age sixty-two. I was sixty-four and she was sixty-three and they paid us back. The reason that we took that was because of her sickness. Blue Cross-Blue Shield would not cover her for her diabetes, or for her heart, and that was four or five thousand dollars.

She was feeling better one day and I said, "Let's go up to the Social Security office."

We went up and got a very nice lady and she got talking to us. She told us that they would pay back to age sixty-two, that we could collect that. The little bit of money that I could get if I waited until I was sixty-five didn't add up. So we both got on to Medicare. I didn't realize that I was getting old till then.

Then about two years after, the construction company that I had worked for, United Engineers, got into trouble down in Florida, and they didn't know how to straighten it. The two fellows that were in charge of the project were two guys that I called ninety-day wonders. They'd just got out of college and they knew a lot of book work but they didn't know actual field work. I had had problems with one of them and I had transferred him. So the company contacted the old super that I had been with so many years, Morris Rogers, wanted him to go down to Florida.

He went down and looked and says, "The only way I'll take this job is if Azel Adams is down with me."

United Engineers called me and told me that they would give me a thousand dollars a week and all expenses until I come back. In the mean time my old buddy come up. I got thinking. I was having trouble with my kidneys.

I says, "I'm not a well man. If I get down there in that heat and get going, I don't think that I'd be the man that you want. I'm not that good right now." So I refused it. He refused it.

They got into some of the biggest lawsuits that the power companies had ever had. They'd flooded out a hundred and sixty-five acres of some of the most valuable land down there that there was.

That's how I happened to get into the stove business. To begin with, the first stove I sold was a Glenwood cookstove and I bought it for fifty dollars. I brought it home and I started wire-brushing it and cleaned it all up, and the grates and linings and everything was good in it. It needed a little welding done, and I did that. I set it out the yard and I put $150 on it. A fellow come and he bought it.

Here it was in September. This Loring Hammer had the auction house in Richmond Corner. I went out there and he had seventeen stoves, heaters and cookstoves, all antique, all in one pile beside the auction house. And mad! He'd moved them from one place to another and hadn't sold any. So I looked them all over, seventeen stoves, and I said, "How much you got to have for the whole of them?"

"Oh," he says, "Make me an offer."

I said, "I'll give you five hundred dollars."

"Oh, can't." he said. "Make it seven hundred and you can have them."

"Well," I said. "I can give you five hundred. I'll take four stoves right now. I'll have the money for the rest in two weeks.

He said, "OK."

I picked two stoves that was really ornate and I just cleaned up and shined them, didn't chrome them or anything, and I sold them for five hundred dollars. They went down to Connecticut. So I went on from there.

I went out and got the rest of them. Some stoves I lost money on. Forced to take back or give money back or something. I'd rather do that than have the customers dissatisfied. I tried to let everybody look over and know what they were buying and I tried to make the stove what it should be.

So this is the way our life has been. I never went for welfare and I never went for unemployment or anything in my life. A lot of people say, "Why don't you get food stamps, why don't you get this, why don't you get that..." I'd rather die. But that is not to say that we never had help. We did, but it was different in those days.

Today you got food stamps, you got welfare, you got everything else. We didn't have any of that in those days, we had nothing like that. And there was probably thirty-five, forty families in the area of The Forks. I recall in our own family, when father was first taken sick, everybody had the flu, it took a long time to come back, you know. You wasn't doing anything, you wasn't cutting any wood, you wasn't earning any money, you wasn't trapping or you wasn't guiding. My father would have been trapping, but he couldn't, he didn't have the strength. So that was a setback in our family. We were poor anyway.

Father went up to the local store and he says to Mr. Holway, he says, "I'm going to have to have some help. I've always paid you, but I don't know just how soon I can get the money back to you, Mr. Holway."

Mr. Holway says, "We've never let you down and we aren't going to now."

Father got enough stuff to get by, but of course it still was a worry. But in those days Mr. Holway knew. He was better than a welfare person looking after people and everything. He knew everybody's troubles. So what would he do? He'd get hold of some of the busybodies in town and say, "Well, they're having it kind of hard and it's a big family and the basic food is a problem for them. They got plenty of potatoes, but they need some sugar, they need some molasses and stuff."

So the townspeople would get together what they called a pound party, that was just the name of it, and everybody in town would come and bring something for the family. And it would be a surprise party. They'd bring all of their kids and have a big hell of a party. They gave us one. This particular day they came to my mother and father was in the spring of the year and it was warm enough to be outdoors. I was probably eight, nine years old. Well, this makes friendship. You love your neighbor that way and you learn to live and love. So that neighbor gets in trouble, you have a big party for him. And I dare say, that the parties came often when it was really necessary. It was more or less, "now it's his turn." There was nobody fighting. Everybody was friends. But you don't live that way today. You meet your neighbor on the street and they don't know you.

It went on right up until about the time I was married. When automobiles come in heavy, things begin to change. Jealousy. New faces come in, didn't want to work with the ways we'd always done, so the old ways was given up. They tried their ways and it don't work. So what did they do? The government takes care of them today. We didn't have Medicare, Medicaid or anything. We suffered it out, but I don't think the suffering was as bad as it is now. Now you suffer from the bills. There're too many people and too many people don't want to work.

We had to move a lot, do without, but we've made it our way. Now we've got to figure a way to get out of this old world. I wanted to be cremated and she says, "No way." She says if I die first I'll never be cremated. So I'm negotiating now with a taxidermist to see if he can stuff us and mount us and give one of us to my daughter and one to my son.

Mrs. Adams: We went up to Augusta one day, shopping, and we came back by Nielson's Taxidermy Shop. So he was gone in there quite a while, and when he come out I says, "Now what in the world did you go in there for and stay so long?"

"Well," he says, "I wasn't going to tell you but you act mad, so I'm going to tell you now." He says, "When we die, I am going to have him stuff us like they do a deer's head or what have you, or a fish, and you can go to Terry and I'll go to Donna. They can stand us in a corner for a hat rack."

And he was serious!